HOW FAR
Will I
RUN

A MEMOIR

HOW FAR
Will I
RUN

CHRISTINA BAIRD

Published in Vacaville, CA. by Little Wing Connections
(707) 738-9962

https://www.facebook.com/howfarwillirun

Michael Kendrick, Photographer
MK iPhotography

http://www.mkiphotography.com

Wendy VanHatten, Editor
VanHatten Writing Services

http://www.vhwritingservices.com

Kevin Iriarte, Cover Design

http://www.Kevin7.com

Ginger Marks, Layout
DocUmeantDesigns

http://www.DocUmeantDesigns.com

Printed in the United States Of America
ISBN-13: 978-0-9891398-0-9 (paperback)
ISBN-10: 0-9891398-0-8

RAVES

"Christina captured my attention immediately! This was a 'I can't put it down' experience. It was wonderfully written with optimism felt behind her every word. What an extraordinary woman she is with an incredible talent for telling her truth. I would love to hear her upcoming story as I'm sure the ending will be as joyous as the journey. Thank you so much for sharing. So generous of Christina for letting us in!"

E. Michele Samson , CSA/Co-Founder
Senior Care Authority

"Christina's words of wisdom are a firm foundation to empower us to really see that life does not allow for excuses. That life is about choices. Regardless of where you have been, what you have been through learn from those experiences and choose to make a positive from a negative. Only then do we truly begin to love ourselves and enjoy life to its fullest."

Don McDonald
Business entrepreneur

"After reading Christina Baird's book I was moved by her writing and her stories. It is very raw and she didn't pull any punches in explaining her life experiences. Today, most of society tries to sugar coat the reality and people only receive some of the truth. I feel this book will help those who are still in the dark. She is to be commended."

David Cook McCall
Movizine, CEO

"Christina's fearless stance is held with calm and poise as she shares her life through each page of this amazing book. Written as only a true warrior could. Thank you for sharing the passion that burns so freely within you with each of us. A book that shines a bright light on the path that reunites our hearts with our souls."

Betty Jo Billick

"The memoir by Christina Baird is one of those books that grabs onto you. Once I started reading about some of her earliest unpleasant memories, I couldn't stop reading – I wanted to know, how does somebody go from abuse and neglect at such an early age to write an enlightening, heartbreaking and inspiring story? This book made me look inside myself and ask this question: Am I using my own experiences to fuel a life which is purposely fulfilling? Or as Christina puts it: 'Holding onto their stories as a means for living in their now.*' Christina's story is one that everybody should read. It is proof that we hold the power to choose our destiny."*

Amy Tarleton Cline

"Reading Christina's memoir reminded me of how fortunate I have been. Also coming from an Italian family, I had two parents at home at dinner-time most every night which certainly helped all six siblings and I to operate with most of the skills needed for a stable life. It's a sobering reality to see what happens when that is not the case, when a child is left to grow up by herself and is forced to withstand the abuse and denigrations of parental figures who are adults in name only.

"The memoir is a harrowing tale of molestation, neglect, substance abuse and misfortune plaguing the life of a young girl starting in early life and lasting into her mid-twenties. It is a brazenly honest account of mistakes and maladaptive behavior that on several occasions is nearly fatal for Christina and her friends. She is an amazingly brave woman to openly chronicle her memoir and to take

the steps needed to correct a hell-bent life that seemed to be running out of time. As a friend, counselor and fellow writer I am so pleased that she has found the strength to tell her story and to live the changes made. This book is about redemption, forgiveness and the will of the spirit and would be helpful to anyone, especially any woman, who has traveled a similar path and needed some inspiration."

Nick Cittadino
Counselor & Instructor
Solano Community College

"A candid account of one individuals unwavering courage and resilience through some of life's most difficult challenges, Christina's determination and grace brings her to a spiritual enlightenment that allows her to love and forgive."

Darren Samuelson

DEDICATION

"To each and every soul that has come into my life and given me the opportunities to grow."

FOREWORD

We are all exactly the same, and yet totally different!!

I am from an ultra-conservative family of nine children where I grew up lost in the shuffle and was thankful for the free lunch program at school as a child. I learned at an early age that I'd have to take care of myself. My father used to tell me, "Edie, don't ever be afraid of working too hard." And then at age 15 my best childhood girlfriend got pregnant. It forever changed both our lives, but that is a different story for another time.

Upon meeting and getting to know someone it's often difficult to see who they really are or what events have molded them into the person they've become. In an effort to fit in, we become trained to show our polished shiny side, giving the illusion that everything is 'fine'.

However life is made up of experiences and choices. For every choice there is a consequence. These create us, mold us, and refine us often leaving us with a tattoo like an artwork of scars. Some scars are obvious and can be seen with the naked eye, and some fade with time and are no longer noticeable. Others run deep and can only be detected when we wince from the pain of the scar tissue built up deep within.

Christina's story is raw, filled with experiences that trigger deep emotion. It touches a part of life I thankfully have had little knowledge of. And, yet in casual conversation early on I recognized something that Christina and I shared growing up . . . we both experienced true unconditional love!

Upon further review we also share a kaleidoscope of results from our life experiences . . . love, patience, understanding, long suffering, God's grace, the desire to love and to be loved, a will to survive, and yes the ability to have and share unconditional love.

Christina's story shares hope, dreams attained and the continued challenge of this adventure we call life.

Edith Thomas, a non-profit professional working with intellectually/ developmentally disabled adults for over 20 years, is currently the Executive Director of "Connections For Life" in the greater Bay Area in California

Acknowledgments

Special Thank You to Wendy VanHatten

I met Wendy at my January luncheon in 2010. At that time I had been taking a break from completing my book, as the chapter I had just finished brought up some unresolved feelings that had really taken me aback.

When I was introduced to her, and found out what she was doing for her life work as an editor, I responded with, "I knew you would come to me when I was ready."

Since that day, Wendy has been patient with me through this daunting, healing process, gently coaxing me, guiding me to keep moving forward and to clean my fish bowl regularly. Wendy VanHatten is an amazing woman, whose strength has been my pillar. She has understood my objective to not blame or indulge in any form of victimhood, yet staying on course to show my childhood as I remember it in my truest form. She has repeatedly asked me who I was trying to speak to throughout my chapters so that she could refocus her projection into the eyes of Gods great gift, our conscious choice that we all have been given. Her wealth of knowledge has kept me in alignment as she kept emotionally unattached to my words FOR me so that this completion is here for you today to read.

Thank you, Wendy, for all that you are and all that you are doing for your community.

I am now aware of all the blessings that I have received in my lifetime. I am grateful for all of those who have stopped and shared a moment with me. I am honored to have experienced such precious moments with each and every one of you. Thank you for your insights.

My Boppa , Lisa Hernandez, Lisa Waud, Derek Collins, Rudy Gonzales, Nils Michals, Nick Cittadino, Paul Accomazzo(Dad), Angela Accomazzo(mom), Uncle Joe, My love, Keith Michael, Isabelle Choiniere-Correa, Corina Urtiaga-Michael, Michael Kendrick, Oshell Kendrick, Margaret Abel-Quintero, Jocelyne von Strong, Joe Saitta, Amber Morton, Kanta Masters, Dennis Holtz, Sabrina Boyd, Myriam Etchegoin, Janina Billick, Karen Winter, Mark Acasio, Gilbert Acasio, Edward Acasio,Don McDonald, Kevin Iriarte, Michelle Purugganan, Selena Tucker, Michelle Andrews, Shawna Dunn, Clairisse Daniels, Mary Shideler, Tony Evjenth, Heather von Arx, Shane Hawkins, Melissa Damelio, Corey Piro, Heather Bush, Jon Michaelsen, Desi Burningham, Deonne Montoya, and Don Young.

THE ANGELS HAVE ALWAYS BEEN HERE

Sitting there in the front row of her classroom, the weight from my head on my folded arm was quickly dissolving deep into the fake wooden desk beneath it. Watching my Señora write my life story in Spanish for my class assignment on her dry erase board, I wondered why it was so hard for her to understand.

She stood staring at me perplexed, stymied, and asking me, "I'm sorry Christina, this just doesn't make sense. How can this be?" Continuing on in her rich Spanish drawl, "Christina, this wasn't a normal childhood. This was just not right, you know?"

Reiterating once more, "Señora, this is what I knew. I never knew anything different. Can you see now how I am having problems translating this?"

That was my childhood, no matter how fucked up my parental figures were. This was all I knew. I had let go of my attachment to that story some time ago and had already rewritten my script. No longer was I the victim. I now had a simple appreciation of life.

1

A few days later, while I was waiting for a class to start, I overheard two young girls talking about their babies and some of their needs. Impressed with their interest for bettering their educational status, I asked them what their reasons were for going to school. They looked as if they were still in high school. In reality, they had just graduated from high school and both had newborns. One commented that she didn't care what kind of job she got as long as it paid for diapers for her baby. Her friend fervently agreed with her adding that they weren't getting much help from their 'baby's daddies'.

This stopped me. Catching my breath, I gasped, "No, no, no. . . . Ladies, you are so magnificent. At your age you've accomplished graduating from high school, brought another being into this world, are working, and obtaining a college degree! How old are you? "

Bewildered, they both confirmed they were seventeen. Rolling their eyes, they grabbed their bags, and walked away. I sat there deflated, watching them enter their classroom and glance back to make sure I wasn't going to stalk them.

I envisioned taking these girls for a run. Yes, a run. Hearing them kick and scream that a mile would be an impossibility, watching them finish their lap with grace and ease, and then proposing to run two miles with me the next day, only to hear the same objections. The next day taking them out again, doubling their run, and listening to their protests yet again.

Both times I would be mesmerized with their triumphs as they would be focused on how crappy it was that I was MAKING them run.

I flashed back to the first time I made it around Spring Lake beginning at Howarth Park, dashing around the border of Anadel, looping through the hilly bike paths surrounding the lake without stopping once. Before, I had only run at the track or counted blocks around my house, never thinking that I could achieve so much more. Experiencing the freedom of my own expanded realizations that my previous runs were not only attainable, but easily accomplished with every new mile reached another one appeared ready to be conquered. I quickly became engaged in seeing how far I could go, how far I could push myself. The more I did, the easier it became to go even farther.

As I came to back to the focus of a class I was now late for, I realized that a countless number of women my age (I was in my early thirties at that time) and younger were holding onto their stories as a means for living in their 'now'. In my twenties, I used my saga as an excuse for my rage and resentment toward others. Looking back, I don't know why I depended so heavily on my narrative since it never really got me too far.

As I sat in class, I realized I needed to write my story, clear of any attachment or judgment. I knew I was raised the best way my family knew how, given the circumstances that were presented to them. I also understood that indulging in this writing meant sliding back into the murky fish bowl of shit that became comfortable for so long to many of my relatives, as well as to me.

So this is my story; the awakened version of my blessed childhood as I have chosen to see it. My time to clear my view of my so called 'shitty deal' I was dealt was not going to go away until I dealt my cards all over again and CHOSE a better hand for myself. Now, I look back at my childhood and I realize that it was the perfect one for me because it was mine and I lived it in my ideal way.

God has given me 33 years to figure this out at my most faithful time. I was presented with an opportunity to see my miracle at the end of the day and I have taken it frantically. It became apparent that it was no longer an option to continue living in a fear that was eating at me and destroying any relationships around me, especially my most important connection, my son, Christopher. I remember yelling at him at the top of my lungs for not listening to me one day, catching myself as I looked down at his big brown eyes, confused. His bewilderment froze me in so much shame that I knew I had to stop living in my self-induced chaos.

My editor asked me who I was hoping to talk to in this book. My answer is this. If just one person in this lifetime can be empowered by my conscious choice to rewrite their own dialogue in their heads, to calm the destructive chatter that intimidates all of us from within, and to not give in to the illusion of victimhood where only the 'lucky' are meant to have a 'dream' life, then I will have succeeded in my intention here.

What I have realized through my continuous work is that I was already and had been for a while living my dream life. I am my product of my childhood and I have made my greatness out of it.

That is all that matters to me and this is my destiny.

THE BABYSITTER

He jacked a little bitty baby
The man has got to be insane
They say the spell that he was under the lightning and the
thunder knew that someone had to stop the rain.

"Janie's Got a Gun" by Aerosmith

This is the cream. I put it on you and I put it on me. See? This will make it easier. It will make you feel good. You'll see. It won't hurt." He perversely nods his head as he instructs me of his task.

He is really tall and skinny with not as much facial hair as my nanu or my uncles. African American, he seems younger than my mom and Uncle Joe. His pants are open and he is stroking his penis. The white cream is folding over his big dark skinned thumb and two toned index finger with the rest of the unabsorbed lotion protruding through his other fingers. He is motioning for me to come over to him with his head.

I look at him confused. I can't talk because I barely know how to yet. I have a dress on, a cloth diaper, rubber pants, and my little leather sandals that are never buckled. When I followed him into his backyard, he turned around repeatedly, held his finger to his lips, and very faintly whispered to me. We are on the side of his house. I am wobbling on the rocks and trying to abide by his shushing me. Near the side fence that separates his backyard from Nana's yard, we are amongst the wild weed stalks and sticky dandelion patches.

He is by the PG&E meters on the cement, just inside his side gate. Bikes and old tires lay strewn between us and we are hiding, creeping, and staying down low. That is why he has brought me here. No one can find us. This is a secret and he lures me to get me to follow him here. Yet, I do not see the candy he promised and dangled in front of my nose to get me to stand where I am now.

I am not that close to him. There are a few feet between us. I can see his full body though as he is bending over caressing himself. I am watching him use the white tube with the big dark lettering on it. The cream is very white and it looks like the cream my grandmother puts on my bottom when she changes my diaper.

I hear my uncle Joe call me, I lose my balance on the rocks, and stumble forward.

"Chris! Christina, where are you?" at first it's real faint and distant. He is in my nana's house and I can hear him open the back screen door and call out to me. His voice is now louder. I look up and startle the teenage boy, who immediately tries to grab at me while adjusting his pants and getting rid of the cream. I charge towards him and the gate, finding my voice, and screaming as loud as I can.

This scares the boy and as I start pounding on the gate, he opens it for me. His hands are full of white lubrication, his eyes are open wide, and a scared look covers his face.

My nana is calling me now, too. Her strong, deep voice is getting louder. Uncle Joe is outside now, just over the fence. I start crying louder and louder. I run across her front yard as fast as I can. Uncle Joe picks me up and asks me what's wrong. My head is in his chest and Nana is grabbing me from him.

"What is wrong with her? Why is she crying so hard?"

I wake up, like a million times before, always ending at the same spot. This dream comes to me on a regular basis and it seems so real to me. I have had it so often that this young man's hands are familiar to me and the dark color of his penis is engrained in my mind. I don't know how I get alone with this kid or how I get back to my nana and Uncle Joe so quickly and safely. Doesn't Uncle Joe see this kid? Doesn't anybody? Where is my mom?

Finally in my early twenties, when the dreams came to me more frequently and I was drinking excessively with my friends, I figured out who the teenage boy was. I was rummaging through my mom's refrigerator one day looking for any leftovers that qualified as a cooked meal. My mom was babbling about the house she grew up in on Mildred Avenue in Pittsburg, California and how different the neighborhoods were back then. I had spent the first three years of my life there until she married Bill and we moved out with him and his three boys.

My nana was pretty much my sole caregiver until we moved. My mom had me when she was 17 and she was not ready "to be my mother", a reoccurring mantra I had heard more than once in my life already. The neighborhood was full of families that had children all about the same ages and we all grew up together. Both my uncles were in the military and were coming back and forth from their assignments. My grandfather, or Nanu as I called him, was a bartender and active in the union which made him rarely home at nights. My mom's sister, my Sisi, was married and had moved out to start her own family. My nana was a waitress, ran the house, and was my savior. My mom came and went since she was still a teenager.

"There were a lot of different Filipino families on Mildred." She went on, and "That's where I would go eat lumpia and adobo all the time. There was a Mexican family that made the best tamales and had the spiciest food. My mouth would be on fire and my eyes would water. I loved it. Uncle Joe and Uncle Mike hung out with the boys from the Filipino families."

"What about you and Sisi? Weren't you friends with the girls on the street?"

"Sisi stayed in the house since she was more of a homebody and older than me. She married Uncle Bob and moved out when I was still a teenager. Yeah, I did hang out with some of them, but mainly with the older kids though, across town. That's what got me in trouble. I hung out with Bill and his friends. He had already been married and had kids when I met him. I was still a teenager." She boasted.

"There was a black family that moved in next door to Nana when you were born. One of the teenage boys babysat you. He was a good kid. He helped out a lot with you. Back then it was common for kids in the neighborhood to just to go out and play and at each other's houses. Nana would call for us to come home when she needed us. She did the same with you. You weren't shy. You just went with anyone . . . Lord knows you have never been shy." She cackled making herself laugh.

"What did you say?" I asked, trembling. I stopped my scavenging, "Mom, what did you say about the teenage boy?" She was out on the front porch smoking and I went and sat next to her. She had been talking to me through the screen door.

"One of the teenage boys watched you a lot when we still lived with Nana on Mildred. He really liked you and he was a very nice kid. Why?"

My dream suddenly became a vivid memory with all the pieces I had sometimes forgotten when I had awakened. I saw his face clearly, "It's real. It wasn't just a dream . . . Mom, that kid touched me too!"

She pulled out another cigarette and started chain smoking as I told her what I thought was a dream up until then. As I was telling her, she eerily filled in my blanks. She explained how trusting Nana was in the neighborhood and how all the mothers on the street helped each other out by watching everyone's kids when they were playing outside. My mom and her siblings grew up on that street, free from any danger or worries.

"Yep, that was him," she said convinced by my description, "Christina, I never knew . . . None of us knew. He seemed like a sweet kid. It never even crossed our minds that anything like that was happening. You were the only baby in the house . . . We were all coming and going . . .

THE PIGGY BANK

And on my easel I drew
While I was thinking of you
And on the roof of my head
In came my five string serenade

"Five String Serenade" by Mazzy Star

I was about three years old when I was first exposed to my
mother's struggles with depression. My mother married Bill,
who I thought was my biological dad until I was about thirteen.
We moved in with him and his three boys in Pittsburg,
California.

Short lived the first time, she divorced him when I was five.
When I was seven she remarried him and divorced him again
when I was eleven.

Our house was a tall, white, wood paneled duplex with a
studio apartment below. We lived in the top of the house that
overlooked the street with a long, steep driveway to the right. In
the front of the house was an oversized stairwell with large,
wooden banisters on each side that frequently served as my own
personal jungle gym. From the street you couldn't tell there was
a house underneath because of the monstrosity of the stairs
covering the front and leading up to our front porch. The

driveway, along the right of the house, was so steep that our old, fake wood-paneled station wagon scraped the rear bumper whenever we would go on family outings. This concrete slope was where my brothers were usually found, flying down the precipitous incline with their bikes, barely dodging oncoming traffic.

I loved making perfume in my little room at the back of the house. Rose petals from gnarled untamed bushes along the driveway were my favorite smell. A surplus of petite bottles, once filled with cheap musk, were now crammed with smashed rose petals in water. These precious containers decorated my tattered, little dresser. This was the only time I lived with my older brothers.

"They took my bike!" I tattled to Bill.

"Tell them to come here," he sighed.

In my snotty disposition, I walked up to all three of them, "Daddy wants you. You're in trouble for taking my bike." As they walked up the driveway with their pissed off looks, they approached the steps of another tall stairway toward the kitchen. Now, they questioned one another . . . why did they have to have me around in the first place? I rode off on my bike, full of smiles, relishing in the satisfaction from the diminutive attention I had just received.

One night at our tall, white asylum, my mom and I were the only two at home. I had been busy in my room making my latest line of fragrance for the week when I was suddenly interrupted by a belligerent commotion at the front door. I answered the door to my aunt frantically pounding on its glass windows, yelling at me to open up. Behind her were numerous police men and paramedics. She stopped in front of me. The others trampled in past us and throughout the house to look for my mom.

"She's going to be okay", my aunt said grabbing me and hiding my confused little body in her hugs, keeping me distracted from the outbreak of chaos that had just spawned around me.

Bustling back and forth, policemen were all over our house. An ambulance had just pulled up and was waiting for them to bring my mom downstairs. Whirling red lights flashing through the front room window overpowered any existing lights in the house. In all the brightness, I was unable to find my mother. Uniforms whizzed by me, too fast for me to comprehend all their commotion. I didn't see them take my mom out of the house. They kept my tiny body covered under arms and wet faces.

After a while our asylum filled with my aunts and uncles, whispering under their breaths. Who would take me home with them?

"I'll take her with me. She can stay at my house," my aunts deliberated with my nana.

"Where is everyone?" All of a sudden they realized no one else was home except for my mom and me when she tried to kill herself in her own bedroom, while I was busy playing in mine.

A year or so later, my mom and I were living in the city. She was going through her first divorce with Bill when she checked into an inpatient insane asylum for her ongoing depression. My mom's sister, my uncle, and my grandmother took me to visit her while I stayed at my aunt's house until she got better.

The hospital was big and pallid. Everything was white. Nothing was on the walls and the halls were long and extremely tall. No people were around except for a random family passing through on visiting hours. The silence in the building was the type of still quiet. It was louder than the gentle rustling from the friction of a nurse's pantyhose when she walked or the mumbling direction given from a consulting doctor.

The bright fluorescent lights projected a sterile state of frigidity in the room where my mom was. We were sitting at a long table visiting with her. I was sitting across from her, while the adults were talking. I didn't listen to them or even care to comprehend what they were saying. She had made a pink piggy bank with magenta flowers painted on it for me. The pastiness of the room was all that I could see. That and my piggy bank.

The little pink skeleton was small and cold and its flowers were made of four circles with a stem, like one doodles on paper when they don't know how to make a distinguishable flower, like a rose or an iris. The brushed pink and blotted, purple flowers have never cracked or peeled except for a tiny chip along the top slit where my movie ticket stubs have been crammed through. The brush strokes are obvious, still permeated through the hardened clay of hollowed insides, filled with memories of my little escapes into happy endings and perfect families that I have seen on the big screen.

The piggy bank was, and is, the only present my mom ever made for me. That petite carcass was meant to be filled with tiny fortunes for future fulfillments.

Instead, it is my only "I love you" note, strategically placed in my Charlie's Angels lunchbox with my little heartfelt endearments of my childhood.

I still have it. I have never broken it to find a countless amount of change saved up, because there was never any change in the house. Any money we did have was used for food, or cigarettes, or anything else an adult uses for appeasement or consoling. Instead it is filled with tickets stubs from movies I have gone to throughout my life.

Only two are ones my mom and I saw together, *The Goonies* and *Back to the Future.*

ELEVEN CENTS

Well she's walking through the clouds
With a circus mind that's running round
Butterflies and zebras
And moonbeams and fairy tales
That's all she ever thinks about
Riding with the wind.
When I'm sad, she comes to me
With a thousand smiles, she gives to me free
It's alright she says it's alright
Take anything you want from me,
anything.

"Little Wing" by Jimi Hendrix

G o get a head of lettuce," Mom barked out at me while I was in the middle of serving my winning game of Four Square in our driveway.

I didn't dare finish it. And, my friends didn't want the crazy lady coming out yelling for everyone to go home because we were ignoring her again. Julian took his red ball and ran off with the others to their court as my mom walked out. She gave me a handful of pennies from the old Alhambra water bottle full of change that always stayed next to her bed. "Hurry, cuz dinner is almost ready."

Bill was gone again, taking with him the latest old station wagon beater that he hadn't crashed yet. He had been gone for about a month this time. When he would leave, we went from poor to desolately poor. Big pots of beans were stewed, rice was steamed, and heads of lettuce slathered with mayonnaise, salt, and pepper. This was a common dinner at the Acasio household. Rationings from the food bank and food stamps kept us going until he came back, most of the time without the car, because it had been impounded or totaled. Even though his jobs were random, once he got back there was a period of mending burnt bridges with his employers who he had walked out on. And, once again we needed to acquire a new car. We would then start eating real food again. Meat, liquid milk, and white cheese made their way back to our table. For a moment, the powdered milk, big blocks of orange cheese, Kix's, and the rice and beans dinners went away.

Walking to the store for my mom was a common past-time of mine, starting as early as first grade. A note was written and change was handed over to me for cartons of cigarettes, stamps, milk, groceries, or whatever my little arms could carry. Short cuts were common as I ran along creek beds and fields, over and through fences, scaling rooftops, and slithering under bushes. From our duplex on Atlanta Court, my desired route of choice to the Lucky's grocery store was over the abandoned ladder set up against the wooden fence behind the apartment buildings at the back end of the cul-de-sac. Dropping down into the field next to the creek bed I waded through buckets left over by various neighbor kids. Most were filled with silenced crawdads and frogs forgotten until the next day's excavation.

Following the creek down the kid-made paths, worn from our rigorous bike riding, I made it to Franquette Avenue. If the gate near Montgomery High School's track and baseball fields was locked, then climbing over the chain link fence was not a crisis. Walking through the field seemed like a trek. The track to my left was colossal, lined with soaring metal bleachers on either side. Baseball fields ran along Franquette Avenue, down to the tiny bridge, crossing the creek to Spring Creek Drive, and running its width to the black top behind the high school. Next to the gymnasium was a wall enclosed by a chain link gate. I could climb the gate, walk along the wall, scale the pole attached to the adjacent building, and hoist myself up to the roof surrounding the quad.

Sitting on top of the world, looking down onto halls of classrooms, I ran on top of each corridor jumping over various levels of tar and tiny pebbles. Sometimes I would warm my back laying on them, basking in the dying sun, watching the clouds turn their bright pinks and oranges.

Realizing my return time with the lettuce was moving fast, I would find new ways to jump down. Picking up my pace, I didn't want to be grounded.

Scurrying down Hahman Drive and into the familiar grocery store helped me to regain some of my time back. Grabbing the first iceberg I saw, going to the ten items or less check out, and then sprinting home would be my saving grace. Rounding the end cap only to see the older, heavy set, blonde woman with the long, bright, fuchsia nails, and matching lipstick as the checker halted me as I entered the end of her long line. Hand baskets sat on the floor in front of each person as they kicked them forward every once in a great while. All the other checkout lines were just as long with heaping carts. I was back to losing time.

My check-out lady didn't smile nor did she show any form of patience. She had checked me out before with my handful of coins, welcoming me to her counter with a look of dread. When it was my turn, I put down my lettuce. As I reached into my designer Kmart jeans, with the fake back pockets and the little pockets in the front, all my change spilled out. The copper coins dropped onto the counter and the floor as my bulging fist squeezed out of the petite denim. As I dropped to the floor to pick up my pennies, I glanced behind to the line of customers staring at me impatiently, desperate to purchase their items and get to their own destinations. The heat from their stares warmed the back of my neck and my face burned a vibrant red.

As I looked up, the cashier stood blankly staring at me, anxiously grasping at the rolling, pivoting pennies, slapping them down for my retrieval. Standing back up, wiping away my fluster with the back of my forearm, I haphazardly regained composure. My ten-year-old brain forgot how to count past eleven cents as I scooted my counting pile towards the cashier's extended nail, pulling them towards on her recount. By this point, eye contact was beyond a standard courtesy and an urgency to get me out of her line was her main objective.

Handing me my bagged lettuce with a stale smile and nod was my only send-off.

Running out of the store, down Hahman, through the school corridors, over my fences, through the field, passing the creek, oblivious to the cricket's harmony blaring in my background, I was making up as much time on my retraction of steps as possible. Once home, our poverty feast could begin. By the time I thrust through my front door, the sun was setting and my mom was dishing up plates.

Looking up, she directed, "What took you so long? Hurry up and make the salad."

As she had the extra worry of her husband gone missing again, I cut the head of lettuce in half, saving the remainder in the refrigerator for tomorrow's meal. My mother came over to add the mayonnaise, salt, and pepper.

"Have you found him yet?" I consoled cautiously.

"No," she answered sharply, as she carried the bowl to the table.

Dinner was in silence. After my mom and sister were done eating, a bath was drawn while I did the dishes and cleaned the kitchen. By the time I was done, my sister was in her crib for the night and my mom was locked in her room until morning. I went to bed, hoping our worries would go away with the night and the new light of the morning would bring my mom out of her slump and the stress out of her heart. School was my sanctuary. There was plenty of food at lunch, caring adults that had to smile and be pleasant no matter what, and recess, which meant plenty of running. It didn't really matter if Bill was home or not; my mother still carried her burdens on her shoulder.

A few days later, when I came home from school, Bill was back. My mom and Bill were in the kitchen and the car was not in the driveway. He had wrecked yet another car, leaving us without transportation once again. My mom's face carried a different set of worries when she looked up from a stack of papers on the table and told me to go in my room and do my homework. Bill looked up at me, hung over and tired, gave me a merciful smile, and focused on my mom as she made calls to family members and employers, letting them know he was back safe and sound and everything was back to normal.

SHE WANTED
A BOY

My mistress' eyes are nothing like the sun;
Coral is far more red than her lips' red;
If snow be white, why then her breasts are dun;
If hairs be wires, black wires grow on her head.
I have seen roses damasked, red and white,
But no such roses see I in her cheeks;
And in some perfumes is there more delight
Than in the breath that from my mistress reeks.
I love to hear her speak, yet well I know
That music hath a far more pleasing sound;
I grant I never saw a goddess go;
My mistress when she walks treads on the ground.
And yet, by heaven, I think my love as rare
As any she belied with false compare.

"My mistress' eyes are nothing like the sun";
Sonnet 130 by William Shakespeare

Looking through my baby pictures one day, I noticed that in a majority of photos, my hair was cut short and my outfits veered more on the masculine spectrum. I asked my mom why I looked like a boy. Her answer was objectively simple, "I wanted a boy."

During my pubescent years, it was a common occurrence for her to have my hair cut when I was getting too much attention from the opposite sex. This was her form of punishment. The eighties brought feathered hair, big bangs, and scrungies. All of which I was not privileged to when I was on my mother's naughty list. Mod styles were popular for short hair, which could have saved me but these do's usually required huge dollops of mouse, mounds of gel, or cans of Aquanet, all of which were never in the Acasio budget.

My first and only attempt of journaling in a diary was cut abruptly short when my mother read that I had kissed a boy for the first time. I did not receive the birds and bees talk, reassuring me that I was like any other girl in junior high experiencing the flush a boy can bring to a girl's cheeks the first time they come close enough to feel their breath. My school had provided videos on sex education and menstrual cycles for us girls, starting in fourth grade. That was the degree of my social instruction on how to be a lady and did not extend any further into my household.

My mother always covered up while in the bathroom or when changing. Being comfortable in my body or loving what God gave me was never endorsed. Covering up in the name of shame was encouraged. Pride in the gift of womanhood, strength in the binding of matriachalism, and wisdom in the nurturing of motherhood was not ingrained in me throughout my childhood. It was awkward for me to receive praise or acknowledgement from outsiders, since I wasn't used to it at home. The nurturing I did receive was from my nana but by my school years, time spent with her had dwindled down to only yearly visits. I had grown to dodge endorsements around my mother, as the dread of her resentment was unbearable.

"You're getting too cocky flipping your hair. You're just asking for all that attention. . . " She dialed the neighbor, "She's coming over right now, cut it all off so she can't flaunt it in front of anyone." My mom hung up the phone and ordered me to give her any hair products I had in my room, "You won't need these anymore," she sneered as I handed her my curling iron. Her ranting continued behind me as I slipped out the front door to the once again execution of any trace of my femininity.

The neighbor was waiting for me at her door. When I saw her, I burst into tears. "Oh honey." Wrapping her arms around me, burying my head into her chest, she pulled me in quickly so that no one would see her consoling. Leading me over to her couch, her arms still tightly wound around my shoulders, I sat beside her and cried, my face buried in her chest for as long as I could keep her there. "I'm going to have to cut it soon. She is going to call for you." As she pulled me away from her, looking into my eyes, "I will try to cut it in a way that you won't need product."

Grabbing my hand, I followed her into her kitchen. Long strands of black hair started to fall to the floor soon after I planted my little body into her chair. The slice of the scissors screeched into my ears broadcasting louder than both my contagious sobs and the ones slipping down my hair dresser's cheeks. Her cuts went beyond a bob, even past the point of any recognizable A-line.

"Christina, I am trying, honey," her deflation exasperated in her throaty tone. By the time her phone rang, the locks that used to fall past my shoulders were blackening my neighbor's floor leaving behind a hairstyle an inch or two longer than a crew cut. My neighbor hung up her phone after assuring my mother that the slaughtering had been executed. She coaxed me into her bathroom, directing me with her hands on my shoulders.

My first glance at my head spun me right back into her chest, loud sobs filled her apartment as she held my jerking body upright. "Control yourself," as she firmly straightened me up. "It's gone. There is nothing we can do about it. Honey, you're beautiful."

Her grip became firmer as I shook my head back and forth, crying out, "No, No, No. Look at me, I'm awful," stuttering my inhale.

"Stop. Stop. Stand up straight." She erected me once more.

"It's done; don't let her get the best of you. Here, wipe your face," as she reached for her towel. "Come on, let's do this. You have to. You have no other choice." She sat me on the toilet and wet the towel. As she wiped my face, I started to catch my breath. "If she sees you this upset, she will do this to you again. You have to act like this isn't that bad. That's all you really can do. You have no other choice. Come on, breathe. You have to go back, or she will come get you."

She grabbed both my hands as she knelt in front of me. Her tiny blue eyes magnified through bifocals locked in my puffy, tear stained eyes. With a half-smile she gave my little wrists a shake to stand up and find my way back home.

I went straight to bed, leaving it to the morning to deal with my new image and the unforgiving peers in my junior high. My mom came in to make sure her order was executed. "I called his mother, I told her everything. You are not allowed to talk him anymore," as she walked out. The burning around my neck pulsed up to my ears. The complete embarrassment couldn't be wiped away, no matter how far I stuck my head in my pillow in the attempt to hide my tears.

Keeping my eyes closed, I hoped to fall asleep faster than the headache that was becoming a reality. Knowing that school wasn't going to be kind to me was better than doing no right by my mother. The lesser of the evils was the freedom of the public school system. I wasn't popular anyway, so laying low under the radar was my only chance for survival amongst my peers.

Eventually, I saw the boy. I carried the burden of embarrassment for both of us. He said that when my mom called his house, his mom didn't know what to say. She didn't agree with my mom, but respected her wishes. As he gasped when he saw my hair, it became clear to me that any kind of attention brought negative reinforcement from my mom.

My hair eventually grew out. As long as I knew my place, I got to keep it.

HEROINE

All that time I was searching, nowhere to run to,
it started me thinking,
Wondering what I could make of my life, and who'd be waiting,
Asking all kinds of questions, to myself, but never finding the answers,
Crying at the top of my voice, and no one listening,
All this time, I still remember everything you said
There's so much you promised, how could I ever forget.

"In Too Deep" by Genesis

It was a common occurrence for me to go to work with Bill. For me, getting out of the house was a quest. However, Bill fit the image of my mom's taste for someone else's redemption. And, with Bill's perverted odalisque satisfactions, I'm not sure which was worse.

There was a 7-Eleven® by our house in Bennett Valley where we would stop to get juices and Hostess® Crumb Cakes. Paul, Bill's new found friend, always seemed to be hanging out in front, smoking. I stayed in the truck when Bill ran in, so I don't know how they became friends or what they talked about. Eventually, Paul would catch rides with us and sometimes even go to work with us.

Paul was a lanky, curly haired man in his late forties; or at least he looked like it. With big, black-rimmed bifocals he had a constantly runny nose and a glazed over appearance. He lived

31

with his mom, supposedly, only two blocks from us. We gave him a ride one day when we just happened to see him out in front of his house. The brown, oversized Izod-like sweater with the leather pads sewn over the elbows and the baggy 501s that he seemed to wear every time I saw him carried with them a musty stench that never left. Even with his sloth like exits from the truck, everything still smelled.

Keeping the windows down didn't seem to help either. Bill's truck was older, so neither air conditioning nor defrosting was an option. Paul didn't talk much, just sort of followed. He never talked to me at all and when words seemed to be coming out of his moving lips to Bill, his amplification was closer to a whisper than any pronounced sound at all.

The truck broke down a lot. Paul would get out with Bill every time they needed to pull over and lift up the hood to check the engine.

Bill got this house cleaning job at an apartment complex on West Ninth Street. He was employed to do all the move-outs. The apartments were roach and rat infested which kept me outside most of the time sweeping and dragging garbage bags to the dumpsters. I hated walking into these apartments with black moving walls and coarse fur brushing the tops of my feet. My uncontrollable squeals, frantic two-step, and the shakes had Bill ordering me out of the rooms. He used a broom to whack the floors and any flying pests seeking refuge in his hair or clothes.

Bombing the apartments for half the day and then bagging all the carcasses was the majority of the labor. By the time I would even think about entering the dwellings we were already days into the project. Paul helped Bill clean the apartments while I waited outside for my bags, randomly whacking the broom around and playing with whatever amused me.

One day I realized that I was waiting forever for them to bring me more bags. My curiosity lured me past the front door of one of the units. I called out to Bill, but he didn't respond. I treaded cautiously through the kitchen, breaking through the litter and stiff corpses. Carpet and linoleum peeked out haphazardly, most either stained or burned. He wasn't in the bathroom downstairs and the more I called out for him, the further I was engulfed in the chaotic debris of filth. I bellowed much louder before emerging upstairs. Still no answer.

The reticence was heavier the farther I scaled the filthy stairwell, kicking rubbish to the side, anchoring myself on each new higher step. All the doors were open on the second floor except for the bathroom which I threw open, pushing Bill forward into the sink console. His pants were to his ankles, one knee was propped on the toilet with his elbow resting on it, and he was holding a small bag he was desperately trying to shove in his fallen jeans.

Bill was giving himself a shot as I stormed through the door. He scuffled to finish his injection while bracing himself against the door so the force would propel me backward, fastening the latch. There was a scuffling to lock the door. No words were coherent, but I heard a disorderly clanking.

I flew down the stairs, rustling garbage, creating a new path on the visibly stained carpet. Slamming the front door open, sprinting to the root beer colored truck, I plopped myself in the middle of the bench seat, crossed my arms, and kicked my feet against the underside of the dashboard.

I was there for a while before Bill and Paul came out. We dropped Paul off and drove home in silence. I flung the truck door open when we got home and ran to my room slamming my door shut, not saying a word.

The next time I went to work with Bill, we stopped at the liquor store on the corner of Sebastopol Avenue and Santa Rosa Avenue by Juliard Park. I ran in to get my Apple 7UP and when I came out, Paul was in the truck talking to Bill. I stopped running when I saw him and started sauntering towards the truck. It didn't matter, though because by the time I got to the truck they were getting out and lifting the lid to the engine. Bill told me to wait in the truck as he held the door for me.

After I opened my 7UP, I could see through the crack of the hood that both their hands were moving. I scooted up on the large covered seat and peered intently through the crack the open hood provided. They were opening Ziploc bags and tin foil and exchanging money. I couldn't see through the foil or what was in the bags as much as I could see their hands trying to cover up their transaction, pretending to work on an engine that didn't need fixing. When they were done, I slid back in my seat, Bill closed the lid, and Paul trekked down the street not glancing back. Bill climbed in, commented I forgot to get him his juice, started up the engine, and we clunked down the street.

A couple weeks later, while sitting in the kitchen at the Bethards Apartment, I asked my mom if Bill was gay. She stopped washing dishes and looked at me, like she was going to knock my curious expression right off my face.

"Why are you asking?"

"Is Paul his boyfriend?" I treaded very lightly.

"Who is Paul?"

Her not knowing who Paul was broke down a dam filled with a million questions. I thought I was uncovering a perverted love scandal with Bill and his hooker, Paul. I already saw Bill as a pervert and the money matched what I saw on Miami Vice. At that point in my life, I thought Bill would fondle anything that walked. As I asked more questions, my mom asked me even more questions. Explaining to her what I saw on the counter and in the bags under the hood weeks before brought her to a rage.

"Take me to his house." By now the green box of Kools were out with smoke emanating through the side opening of her clenched lips. Paul was out in front of his house lingering, as if his mom just kicked him out of the house and told him to go play with his friends. I pointed to him. Mom pulled the Buick over, jerked the car in park, and jumped out slamming the door with the car still running.

Screaming at Paul she ran down the street toward him. The steaming rage coming out of this wild woman immobilized me with complete terror. All sound left my ears, my legs had piercing pain, and my body shook. I became gelatinous, oozing into my seat with the seatbelt as my only support.

I saw Paul stop frozen in his pacing, a stupefied terror painted on his face as my mother flew at him like an ostrich trying to take flight. He used his arms to cover his face for protection, shrinking down to my mom's height as she stood in front of him, yelling and screaming. Cowering down smaller and smaller, he tried to avoid her wrath of words, encapsulating him in her fury. When she was done, she came back to the running car, resumed her smoking posture, and I started to breathe again.

When Bill came home that night, he found my mom locked in their room. Once he entered, they didn't come out until morning. My mom told me afterwards that Bill had been a methadone user and that he and Paul were using heroin together. Paul was his drug buddy, not his hooker. In the past when Bill would leave for months on end, it was actually to go on these binges.

Within a month we were both signed up for Al-Ateen and Al-Anon. Bill was seeking his repentance through his local Jehovah's Witness chapter for refuge.

FATHER KNOWS BEST

The quality of mercy is not strained.
It droppeth as the gentle rain from heaven,
Upon the place beneath.
It is twice blessed.
It blesseth him that gives and him that takes.
It is mightiest in the mightiest,
It becomes the throned monarch better than his crown.
His sceptre shows the force of temporal power,
An attribute to awe and majesty.
Wherein doth sit the dread and fear of kings.
But mercy is above this sceptred sway,
It is enthroned in the hearts of kings,
It is an attribute to God himself.
And earthly power dost the become likest God's,
Where mercy seasons justice.

"Merchant of Venice" by William Shakespeare

I can't deal with your mom sometimes, she's just so . . . I can't be around her . . . you know I will take you with me the next time I leave, right?" Bill asked in his most insincere, seductive whisper. I shivered any time I was left alone with him.

"I hate her," I sobbed. "I hate her so much. Please don't leave again. Just deal with her. Please."

He was the only Dad I knew at that time and he had left so often and for so many months, that when he was gone my mom made us ten times more miserable. She lived for him; she would die for him. We all knew this. She was miserable without him yet when he was there she kept catching him doing whatever, which would cause him to leave again. He would go to work one day and by the time I got home from school my mom would be on the phone looking for him again.

"He took the car again and all our money. I have some food stamps left . . . Yeah, I know . . . Let me know if he shows up there. I'm sick of this . . . Yeah . . . I know I can't keep going and bringing him back . . . He's using again. The last time he was binging and he totaled the car. We just bought another station wagon, too. Yeah, I know, you would think they wouldn't have him come back, but they do . . . I know he's a good worker . . . he needs his insulin. I'll call the hospitals . . . Let me know if you hear of anything."

I wiped my nose with my soggy toilet paper wad I had grabbed on one of my escapes from my bedroom in the last three days. It was Sunday night and I was again on restriction by my mom for the whole weekend.

Bill had brought home an old abandoned Army bunk bed for my sister and I that he found at one of his job sites. I was excited to have bunk beds, but not so thrilled with the olive green color even though most of it was chipped off. So, Mom had repainted them white and put them side by side.

He was sitting on the one in the middle of the room. I was on the one against the wall. I was lying down, tired from crying all weekend. Aspirin didn't help the migraines like Mom said they would. My mom was in her room with my baby brother and my little sister. It was a common occurrence to lock herself in her room when she was angry at everything. I suppose she was thinking of ways that she could die and forget about the safety of her children.

My mom was a miserable person who fell back on suicide attempts for attention in my early childhood. She was put in an insane asylum when I was five. Her jealousy for me was disgustingly displayed by her constant attempts to make me look like a boy. As a toddler she dressed me as a boy and kept my hair really short. When I started filling out and getting noticed by young boys, she again had all my hair cut off. Her motto was, "You're guilty until proven innocent." My mom would put me on restriction for weeks. It had become such a regular occurrence that she forgot when I was on or off restriction. In reality, I was always on.

My only two escapes were to go to work with Bill at his cleaning job at the yogurt shop, or his landscaping jobs, or go to school during the week. This meant I was left alone with him once again, giving him ample opportunity to molest me. He knew that calling me a 'tattletale' was enough motivation to keep me quiet.

At first Bill would only fondle my breasts and shove his big nasty hands down into my crotch and grab at it. I would grab at his arms and try to push his hands out while he ripped holes in my tights and ripping off my panties in entirety. But, both my hands wrapped around his forearm were no match for his large

39

forceful thrusts. I tried forcing his arms down, while I squeezed my legs shut. He pushed them open with his other strong arm, taunting contemptuously "If you say anything, no one will believe you. They will just call you a tattle-tale." This was a struggle I never won.

The yogurt shop was the worst because it was at night and we were alone. It was a store front so we would be locked in the back to drain and clean out the machines. His grabbing never stopped and my little body was at his disposal. By then I started wearing a training bra, which he lifted up to get to me. I would squeeze my eyes shut as tight as I could and try to scream. My voice was my only liberator but there was no one around to hear me.

All the free yogurt and M&M's in the world could not placate what happened in the back wash room.

Some nights I would wake up aroused and find him rubbing on my vagina. I would shout in my head, "What are you doing?" at the top of my lungs. But, all that would come out was a meek, scared, trembling whisper, "What are you doing?"

My mom should have heard it. I know she should have. It was loud enough. She chose not to. Bill, startled, would point at some toys across the room and run out.

One day I was having a Bible study with Rita, an older lady at our congregation. We were reading about the word molestation. I had never heard that word before that day. Rita explained, "It's when an adult touches a young person's private areas and does things to them."

I looked down when she said that and got real squeamish. I got that feeling that is still so familiar to me even to this day, between my legs when Bill would touch me. My vagina squeezes together for safety and my body lurches forward. I shake a little and get that nasty burning feeling between my legs that makes me want to scrub down there with a pumice stone or an SOS pad.

Picking up on my fidgeting, Rita asked "Christina, has anyone touched you like that?" I shook my head yes, still looking down, and embarrassed to make eye contact. "Bill?' she asked cautiously.

I knew she was afraid because I could see the terror in her eyes when I shook my head again. Guardedly, I shook yes again.

"I told Tina before that Bill touches me and that it hurts, about a year ago. She told the elders. They said I had to go to them and talk to them about it myself." I said quietly.

Rita stared at me, "Christina, have you told your mom?" Silence.

She asked again.

I shook my head frantically. "No! I'm not telling her!" I started crying. There was no way I was telling her. She wouldn't believe me. She'd be very angry with me. I wasn't going to tell her . . . nuh-huh . . . nope.

Rita grabbed my face and made me look at her, "You have to tell her. I will give you a week. Otherwise I will tell her. You have to Christina. Okay?"

I just stared at her. I didn't say yes or no. I just stared at her with pure antipathy and fear. This was not going to be good. I knew this. I felt it. That night when Rita dropped me off, I knew there was nothing I could say to get her to change her mind. I knew she loved me and I also knew that she didn't know what the hell she was doing to me.

Exactly a week later, Rita started calling my house. Bill took the messages for my mom to call her. My mom asked me what Rita wanted and if she was going to tell her something she wasn't going to like. I distinctly remember my mom's exact words, "Christina, do you have something to tell me? Is Rita going to tell me something that I'm going to be mad at you for?"

The phone rang and I flew to it. It was Rita. "Have you told your mom yet?" came after my quivering hello. "Okay," I whispered and I hung up. I walked into the living room where my mom was sitting on the couch, her legs up, eating. Looking down, I trembled, "I have to tell you something. We have to go somewhere."

My mom looked at me. She saw my face, saw how small I felt, and how frightened I was. She saw this wasn't going to be a good thing in any way and said "Let me get my cigarettes. Get in the car. Bill, we'll be right back," she yelled. I heard her shuffle to the car with her keys and her cigarettes behind me. She got in the car and pushed in the car lighter. She didn't say a word to me. I could tell she was scared. Not mad, just scared, which made me even more scared. I looked out the window as she drove towards Howarth Park. She parked in the upper parking lot facing Lake Ralphine. She pulled out another cigarette and turned to me.

The geese were squabbling in the dirt in front of us near the picnic tables and the ducks were fluttering in the water to the little island near the rocky shore. Runners and bikers were coming down from the trail racing with the daylight. The sun was setting and the weather was definitely cooling down.

The date was February 21, 1984. I was 11 years old and I had been groped and fondled by my dad for the past three years, now for the last time. I was no longer a victim. I was a rival. She looked at me and didn't say a word.

She smoked and stared, "Does this have to do with Rita?" she asked, "What is she going to tell me?" Silence was held out as long as I could take it to before an arm was going to come across the Buick's long bench seat at me.

"Bill touches me," I blurted without breathing. "That's why I kept locking my door, putting the stuffed animals all over my floor, why I kept trying to sleep with my clothes on for the next day, and why I wanted to sleep under my laundry." The words weren't stopping.

Her eyes grew contemptuous while her hand kept raising her cigarette for her inhale. Retracting puffs of grey smoke loomed in the car and slightly, slowly, subtly floated around her head, out her window, through the car, and out my window behind me.

"And he locked himself in the bathroom with that guy Paul at the house on West Ninth. I knocked on the door and they were putting their clothes on when I knocked and tried to push open the door. They were taking things off the counter . . ." My words kept blubbering out. There was no room for questions. "He touches me when he's driving and I pop the clutch out of gear and he says that you will be mad at me if I break the car." I didn't take one breath and I know by looking at her that she stopped breathing also. I stopped and started breathing again.

It was quiet. She pushed in the lighter again. The click broke the silence. I watched the cigarette light up that bright orange as she sucked it to life.

Agitated, she asked me, "Are you sure? You're not making this up? You're not lying? When did this happen?"

"I have a calendar. I mark down every time it happens," I said. This moment, this very moment is when my fear of her, of Bill, and what I thought would happen to me evaporated and dissolved into nothingness.

"I have to go. I have to think about this," she said as she started the car and floored it home. She didn't pull into our apartments. She pulled up out on the street and told me to go over the neighbor's house until she came back. She sped off. I went to the next door neighbor's apartment, whose door was a foot away from ours. By now it was around 7 p.m. or so. I asked the lady if I could wait there until my mom got back. She was so wrapped up in her kids and she was friends with my mom that she really didn't ask me why. She knew my dad left a lot and that my mom was always mad. So it didn't faze her that my dad was next door with the kids and that my mom wanted me there.

My mom finally called around 11 p.m., "Christina, I can't believe I left you and the kids with him. Tell Rosie thank you

44

and meet me out front with your calendars." I ran so fast through my house, ignoring Bill, grabbing the calendars. By the time I got to the street my mom was there with her friend. "I can't believe I left you and the kids . . . " she kept repeating to herself.

The police station was very bright, quiet, and cold. The lady at the desk was the only one making any noise with her typing and her occasional answering and transferring of the phones. The officers that kept walking through the waiting room seemed to silence when they saw me and seemed to walk in even slower motion when they passed me. My mom was at the counter filling out paperwork and checking in. I had this feeling that my mom's friend was the reason why we were there.

My guess was that she went to her friend's house and told her what had happened and the friend convinced her to turn Bill in. I was tired and I was done with my childhood. I felt old, ready to lie down, and sleep my way into heaven. I didn't know at that point what kind of childhood I did want. I just knew I was done with this one. I didn't think about consequences sitting in that questioning chair or as I was being recorded. As I showed the calendars and what the symbols meant, my words just bubbled out like a small gurgling stream running fluidly through the rocks. I don't remember when I stopped talking. The investigators asked me only a couple of questions as they were writing; letting the recording pick up anything they missed.

My mom just sat there and said nothing. She was completely silent. I noticed her picking and biting at her cuticles and again chain smoking. The calendars took a lot of pressure off me on the questioning. When they compared the dates with my mom, she confirmed them to be times that I was left alone with Bill. After what seemed like so many hours, I was done. It was over. The police followed us home to escort Bill out of the house. Apparently, he couldn't be at the house anymore when I was there they told my mom. There was nothing more to say. I never had to go to court because Bill admitted to everything saying, "She acted like she liked it."

When they woke him up and told him to get dressed, he kept repeating, "Why is she doing this to me? Ang, why is she doing this?" My mom didn't answer him. She just kept her head turned away from him. I don't know if they took him to jail that night or where he went but that was the last time I saw him until I was an adult and a mother to my own son.

Bill was sentenced to time in prison and was let out after six months; time served for good behavior. The woman that my mother went to see after I told her was my savior in stopping my abuse. Bill's sister, my aunt and all her family shunned me as well as Bill's religion for going to the officials. Even though Rita was a Jehovah's Witness, and she wanted me to tell my mother, the protocol for the congregation was to go through the elders. Since they had not made it their priority a year before, I wouldn't have opened up to them if my mother had brought me to them. Bill was baptized and was already seeking repentance for his drug addiction, when I went to the police. The elders came and counseled me, as they felt that he was remorseful for his actions and asked me if I was remorseful for going to the authorities instead of keeping it in the church. I was not. My mother and I were not baptized with the witnesses so a 'disfellowship' was not publicly announced. Still, we stopped going to their meetings.

That year SAY, Social Advocates for Youth, had started a program for children to have a safe place to confront their predators and MADD, Mothers Against Drunk Driving had begun to be recognized as another strong advocacy for children. Even though Bill was out of our house, my mother still wanted to save her marriage, through one of the programs that were offered through SAY. My mom and Bill attended a weekly support group for molesters and their families. Before I told about my molestation, the only type of counseling I had was through the Jehovah's Witnesses, SAY, and the courts.

Somehow, during this time, Bill met my friend Heather's mother, started dating, and eventually married her. My mother met a man named Jerry from this group and started dating him. Telling on Bill didn't make my life easier. It made it more confusing, convoluted in a sense. My mother became more physical with me. Shoes and wooden spoons weren't cutting it. Fists and throwing me before kicking me out was becoming more common.

She was going through her divorce while dating another offender, going out drinking with her friends, and leaving me home to babysit with the neighbor kids my age with pizza and rented movies. My determination to get out of the way of her path was growing stronger. So each time she kicked me out, I started making it harder for her to call me back so quickly.

In the midst of my crumbling, unstable household I was introduced to my biological dad, which created a tiny spark of hope for normalcy. Exposing my abuse opened up a variety of wounds that were not healing right in the first place.

When I was 30 years old, I walked into this restaurant with my son's father and my son. Bill was there. He was old and sickly looking, sitting on the waiting bench of the lobby. He seemed so small and feeble. My mom had remarried by then and we were meeting the whole family for breakfast. She was happy for the moment; there were grandkids for her own redemption.

JOLIET

"Great Minds discuss ideas; Average minds discuss events; Small minds discuss people."

Eleanor Roosevelt

B ill isn't your dad. Thia Mary and all her kids are your cousins, but only because I married Bill. Your Aunt Gloria is actually your real dad's sister. In fact, she is his twin."

"Then why do I have his last name?"

"When I married him the first time, I changed your name."

"Did he adopt me?"

"No. You talk to Aunt Gloria all the time. If you want we can ask her for your dad's number."

"What's his name?"

"Tommy"

By this time, I was going to the weekly Al-Ateen meetings. Mom was becoming a regular at Al-Anon, which meant we no longer had to go to the Jehovah's Witness meetings. Neither of us really felt a deep connection with the religion's beliefs. Nor did I feel it was God's real intention to 'disfellowship' anyone because they did not hold up to their end of the arrangement made between themselves and the other imperfect individuals of the congregation. Mom used any excuse in the world to continue smoking and living life on her terms. Bill was diligently going through the process. He had the elders convinced that his agenda was to be clean and sober. I hadn't disclosed his other misconducts to Rita, yet.

At first, finding out about Tommy gave me a little hope of liberation with the whole idea of fatherhood. My Aunt Gloria was a childhood friend of my moms. We had visited with her and her kids throughout the years, so I knew her. I just never knew how I was related to her. She was a beautiful woman with long black hair and strong Mexican, Indian features. Her kids were of mixed race as she was married to an African American man. I don't ever remember meeting him. I just know he existed. They still lived in the town of Pittsburg, where my mom and dad grew up. When I was growing up, I heard the town referred to as "The Pit". Aunt Gloria treated me a little different than Thia Mary, Bill's sister. Maybe it's because I just visited and didn't stay with Aunt Gloria. Maybe I wore out my welcome at Thia Mary's house, considering I stayed there for months on end before I started my schooling. Either way, Aunt Gloria was more nurturing and Thia Mary was more degrading.

Talking to my Aunt Gloria, I found out Tommy lived in Joliet, Illinois. He moved to Illinois after he left high school. My mom only made it to ninth grade so I don't know if my dad made it much further. Mom had me when she was seventeen, due to failed abortion attempts. My dad stayed around my first six months until he went to buy me a pair of shoes I never received.

Now, the only way I would be able to be in contact with him, would be through collect calls from the Joliet Correctional

Center, his home. Aunt Gloria told me that Tommy called her randomly and that the next time he called, she would have him call me. Rubbing it in Bill's face that he wasn't my dad anymore was my sweetest little empowerment. Going down the meat isle at the Lucky's grocery store, my face held the greatest smile. Sneering at Bill, "You're not my real dad. I know about Tommy and you can't touch me ever again or he will kill you."

That was the biggest statement I ever made to that pedophile. His jaunty step went absent, his face was taut, and his hands were whitish pink as he gripped the red handle of the shopping cart. Thrilled, I skipped with glee to my mom in the bread aisle.

For me, Tommy's first phone call was full of hopes of a father in shining armor riding through the phone, rescuing me from my jealous matriarch and the groper. I picked up the phone, "Will you accept a collect call from a Tommy Zaragoza?" Anticipation. . . . Anticipation.

"Hey Christina," elongated into a low rideresq drawl. I pictured Cheech Marin on the other end.

Disheartened, my voice waivered. "Hi Tommy."

"I'm your dad. You can call me Dad. You know, when I left, I went to Bill and asked him to look after you."

"Thanks, Dad."

Our first conversation established my address so Tommy could send me money for the collect calls and for the church women, who visited him, to send me various presents. His calls came weekly and were short. As I got to know him, Bill's addictions and molestations were revealed. Even though there was transition in my little apartment in California, my knowledge of a possible new role model diminished quickly. A father in prison is no better than a father groping you on the outside. It didn't matter that the music players, jackets, cassette tapes, and jewelry were coming on a regular basis.

After a few months, Tommy called and asked to speak to my mother. I heard her say she wasn't comfortable with me flying by myself. Yes, she would be comfortable coming if her ticket was paid for. She handed the phone back to me.

"Mija, the ladies of the church have offered to buy your tickets to come see me and you can stay at their place. Do you want to come?"

"I have to fly on a plane?"

"Yea and your mom said you can come, only if she can come, too."

"Really? She'll let me come?"

"I'm going to see if they can have you come out for a week, so that you can come visit me more than once. The ladies take care of us. The one that sends you all the gifts will put you up in her house. She lives near here and comes all the time."

By then, Bill had moved out of my mom's house and into Heather's moms house, with Heather, her mom, and Heather's little sister. Bill was in heaven.

One of the ladies from the church in Illinois called soon after to arrange our flight and accommodations. We were to stay with one of the ladies and her husband at their house in a town just outside of Joliet. They would take care of everything.

We just needed to bring clothes suited for the Illinois summer heat.

I had never left California, much less been on an airplane before. Stepping off that plane and having the heaviness of the humid continental climate air tuck me in under its thick blanket of moisture definitely went against my agenda to have the biggest hair possible. Aquanet was no match for that weather.

Before we left the airport we picked up another woman coming in from Chicago to visit her husband who was also serving time. Her accommodations were the same as ours. She was a sweet lady with a strong resemblance to Cheryl James, singer from the rap group Salt and Peppa, sporting the wide gold bamboo cut hoops and an a-line hair do with a bleached top layer that swooped to one side. The band was popular at the time. I remember thinking her hair was so cool, defying the humidity and all. Important 80s protocol was the bigger the hair, the better.

After our hostess settled us in to our designated rooms, we were brought into town for dinner to relax and go over our week's itinerary. My mom asked to stop at a liquor store to buy some cigarettes. Our fellow visitor said she needed something, too, so my mom said she would wait in the car and gave me money to run in with our new friend. Before we got up to the register I handed the money to the woman to pay for my mom's green Kools. The man at the counter seemed approachable until it was our turn. Our fellow traveler asked for the cigarettes and put her items on the counter. The cashier returned with the cigarettes and threw them on the counter.

Ringing up the items, he told my friend to place her money on the counter. This startled me and caught my attention. I stopped fiddling with the candy on the attached shelf and focused on what was happening right in front of me. My friend smiled, chuckling a bit, and obliged. The cashier picked up the money, retrieved her change from the register, and threw her change at us, causing the coins to fall over the counter and onto the floor. My friend collected the items while I scavenged on the floor for the rolling currency.

When I stood up, I must have had such a perplexed look on my face. My friend grabbed my arm and yanked me out of the mini mart. A sneer was the only thing audible. She waited until we were in the car to explain to me that in the area we were staying was predominantly racist and that the man did not want to touch her skin in the money exchange.

My concept of racism was that it had ended years before and that in the 1980s it didn't exist. Anger for the ignorance overwhelmed me. Our hostess explained to us that even though she was white, she had grown up in this town and that it was an unspoken subject not to draw attention to one's personal beliefs. People were to live in harmony within her community. This meant not standing up to racists, but to be firm in your own actions and freedoms. She went on to tell us that it was common to overlook the ignorance for personal safety reasons and that losing your temper in public would not force change on others, just attract an excuse to harm one's home and family members.

She asked me to watch my tongue and to abide by the government of her community while I was a guest in her house.

The restaurant she chose for us was a 'meat and potatoes, side of the road, and order at the counter' type. We were chatting amongst ourselves as we walked in. The clanking of the silverware silenced. We watched a restaurant full of people push back their chairs, gather up their children, and line up to pay their bills. No one looked our group in the eyes.

They paid their bills without speaking to each other or to the cashier. The cashier handed over the bill, payment was made, and the ching, ching of the cash register echoed as the door was opened and shut. The herd of customers headed out, emptying the restaurant within minutes. A couple of employees came from behind the counter and started bussing the tables. We had our pick of tables. The man that rang everyone up walked over to us shaking his head. He gave our hostess a look as if begging her to stop killing his business in the future.

With a huge sigh, he took our order. During dinner, conversation surrounded the upcoming week's schedule. Going to the prison at least two days a week was the maximum allowed. Going sightseeing to St. Louis and the Mississippi River were the highlights. Occasionally, an unsuspecting patron would walk through the door and lasso their family right back out again. I didn't say much. In fact, I couldn't say much as my words wouldn't formulate and I couldn't comprehend what was happening. My mother couldn't help clarify what was happening either as she was just as bewildered as I.

The next morning, my mom woke me up before the sun even climbed out of its own bed. She wanted to take a walk so she could smoke. She said she was hoping to catch a breeze or two before the heat weighed down the air. I had washed and dried my hair, adding my usual pound or two of Aquanet only to step outside to find not even a slight whoosh of breeze. My big ball of bangs fell in my face. There wasn't much conversation on that walk. Our awkwardness to that foreign place left us speechless, our minds perplexed on how people survived here without melting or getting hung for cohabitating. By the time we got back, the house was awake. As I sat down to eat my cereal, our hostess started preparing me with the rules of the detention center.

"Christina, don't hand anything to your dad. You can hug him, but not for too long. Listen to the guards at all times. And don't take off any of your jewelry in the visiting room."

Our fellow guest reiterated listening to the guards, sharing that what seemed like strange demands were really for our protection. They made me stop eating and acknowledge their directions.

"Okay. Okay. I got it," I said, slurping the apple cinnamon milk out of the bottom of my cereal bowl.

I didn't value their severity until her car pulled up to the gargantuan stone walls and expanded rolls of barbed wire. Again, I was confounded into silence. The long walk to the first of many doors I was about to go through felt like I was burrowing deeper and deeper, even though the sky above me was high. The first door we entered brought us into a white walled waiting room where all our documentation was taken and reviewed. Our wait wasn't long before we were escorted by our first set of guards through the second door of the concrete labyrinth, where we were searched for sharp objects and drugs.

The officer instructed us on contact procedures. Hugs and pecks were okay. Nothing else would be tolerated and like the ladies said, no exchanges of any kind were permitted. The third door deeper into the prison was the beginning of a series of metal gates. One gate closed, another would eventually open. Our hands were marked with a stamp that could only be seen under a black light. These were reviewed before each entrance through a new metal threshold. The unpainted stone walls grew darker as each corridor unfolded and the absence of natural light was replaced with fluorescents and halogens. Finally, we entered a room full of anticipating inmates who were awaiting their guests. The room was full of tables surrounded by chairs, restaurant style with guards posted throughout.

My dad bellowed out sobbing, "Mija!" as my mom and hostess stood back for my wet bear hug.

My father was a very hairy man. A black braid draped his backside; his mustache intertwined with his flowing beard down the front of his prison issued light blue button-down, covering up his numbers printed underneath his left collar. His knuckles on his hands were hidden by long hairs that grew all the way up his arms. My first and only revolving thought during the introductions was the answer to why my toes were so hairy. Tears streamed down his cheeks, creating sopping hair that dampened the front side of his shirt. At most, my dad stood five foot four in stature. Tattoos covered his hands, arms, neck, and face. His resemblance to Cheech Marin in *Up in Smoke* was uncanny, a result of partaking in too many substances in his years.

His crying became obnoxious quickly, as he walked me to a table covered with picture frames made out of gum wrappers.

"Mija, I made these for you."

These showed me the ways of his world. My mother and our hostess sat back and let us catch up. Our other house guest was on the other side of the room with her spouse, engrossed in her visit. I asked Tommy about all his tattoos, especially the ones on his face and his hands.

"The ones on my face are actions that I had to do in here to stay alive."

He skirted around my questions as to why he had called this place, 'the concrete jungle'; his home for so long. His story was that he went to Illinois soon after I was born, and he acknowledged that he never returned with shoes for me. He got caught up with some type of mafia-related situations which led him to be framed for murders he didn't commit. His life was prison; his language, his demeanor, and his agendas were apparent.

Off to the right side of the room was a wicker chair and couch set up for pictures. A photographer was posted with a Polaroid, taking pictures of inmates and their families. I had pictures taken with my dad and by myself in the big wicker chair. When the pictures dried, he slipped some in the gum wrapper picture frames for me to take home and kept some for himself to put up in his cell. Towards the end of our visit, one of the guards called for our 15 minute wrap-up "Mija, give me your earrings."

I was wearing cheap red colored ball earrings.

"Why?"

"Because I can make money off of them in here. They are cheap you can get more out there. They are worth more in here."

"But they said not to take anything off."

"Just play with your ear with your hand and slip them off."

My mom and our hostess were visiting and weren't paying attention as I fiddled my earrings off, one by one. Tommy grabbed my hands into his across the table, lifted my arms, and gave me a big hug. As I pulled away, I saw him adjusting them in his mouth. Our goodbyes consisted of hugs and kisses and as Tommy reached out to hug my mom, she reluctantly leaned forward only to be greeted with a tight grip and a mouth full of tongue. I said good bye to Tommy and our hostess assured him one more visit before the week's end.

As we were walking down the pathway, towards our car, our hostess hugged me, "I see your earrings are gone, missy."

The rest of our week consisted of being caught in rain storms visiting the Mississippi, walking around the mall in St. Louis, and one more visit with Tommy. My mom stayed back the second time and I lost another pair of my earrings. Our hostess was one of a group of senior women that dedicated their time to the men of the prison that attended their Christian services. My hostess fed us, acted as our tour guide, and opened her house to us for a week. I kept in touch with her, my father, and our fellow house guest until I left my mother's house. Over the years, I have heard through my aunt Gloria about my father's revolving door in the municipal reform system. That's as close as I have chosen to be with my father in shining armor.

SUMMER CAMP

Nature's first green is gold,
Her hardest hue to hold.
Her early leaf's a flower;
But only so an hour.
Then leaf subsides to leaf.
So Eden sank to grief,
So dawn goes down to day.
Nothing gold can stay.

"Nothing Gold Can Stay" by Robert Frost

The Dependent Unit was a place where kids went when their parents didn't want them anymore, or when the courts deemed the children would be safer there until they could be placed into foster care or adopted. The now abandoned housing facility is located in front of Los Guilicos, Sonoma County's Juvenile Hall, on Pythian Road on the outskirts of Santa Rosa heading towards Kenwood.

Large fields of grass surround both facilities leading out to the main highway. Pythian Road serves as a long narrow driveway to both the facilities and also leads to the south entrance of Mt. Hood. Once you pass Juvenile Hall, Pythian Road becomes a rural, tapered road garnished with tall pines, white oaks, and random walls of wild brush. There have been a few abductions and slayings here, including the infamous

Richard Allen Davis' kidnapping of Polly Klaas in 1993. Other than an occasional residence here and there, the two facilities sit in the midst of vineyards, unquestioning hills, and lost back roads.

At the beginning of eighth grade, I befriended a beautiful, perfectly feathered blonde haired girl named Tamy. She had naturally long nails, not acrylics, painted rocker blue. My mom had kept my nails as well as my hair short so I would not draw any male attention, which I apparently was not allowed to have. In turn, this gave me ample opportunities for ridicule from my classmates. I was not allowed to have the Farrah Fawcett look, wear any bright colors on my nails, nor wear any black clothing. Tamy and a few other kids rode a bus in from the Dependent Unit. She hadn't seen her parents in a while, and was living at the DU until a foster home opened up for her.

Tamy had this amazingly engaging smile and big blue eyes that exuded warmth and humility. Her confidence, gained through her childhood opportunities, fueled her survival instincts to be genuine, not allowing her to feed into the frivolous drama that took place in typical junior high schools. We had similar backgrounds, yet she danced around the topic of who her abusers were and what brought her to me at Herbert Slater Junior High in 1985.

It was obvious that we followed the same stride of our own reality and an advanced disciplinary spectrum that was much stricter than that of our fellow classmates. Beatings from my mom's hefty wooden spoon, which she often broke on me, were inevitable. Tamy's legal guardian; court appointed supervision.

We had no wiggle-room for being kids and enjoying extra-curricular activities.

Tamy was considered a rocker and was accepted on the west side of the snack bar during brunch and lunch breaks. She seemed to have a large variety of clothes thanks to the donations left for the girls at her residence. I, on the other hand, had my five outfit rotation that I embarrassingly acquired by shopping with my mom at Kmart and the Lucky's grocery store in our neighborhood at the beginning of the school year. My J'Espere[1] t-shirt was the highlight of ridicule for one of the rich preppies in my P.E. class, who cornered me and interrogated me in front of the rest of the class one day

"Where did you get such a cheap shirt? Probably Kmart. I bet you she doesn't even know what that means," she roared as all the rest of snobs looked down from their giant pedestals and gave me their scum of the earth looks. The wanna-be's laughed, as they tried to fit in. With my face turning clammy, sweaty, and red, I held back my tears as Tamy opened up our locker and hid me behind her,

"Seriously, Christina, her boyfriend says she smells like fish. He's telling everyone, bragging that she is a shitty fuck. Don't let her get to you."

In the eighties, MTV was not free with basic cable. My Pee-Chee folder proclaimed that I loved bands like Depeche Mode and Duran Duran. Tamy's professed her love for Metallica and Motley Crue.

---

[1] French translation, I really hope not.

The same preppy found me again, this time in history class. "Tell me your favorite song from Depeche Mode." Tamy stood behind her, mouthing the names of songs they sung but I couldn't figure out what she was saying. My snob bully grabbed my folder from me, and with her pen scratched out my Depeche Mode. She pivoted around sharply and headed for the door mocking me to her followers as they scurried behind her with their shrill laughs. Tamy sat with me, both of us deflated . . . slouched in our chairs. We both stayed very quiet as the room cleared out and Mr. Weil, our teacher, began to tell us to "Rapido, Rapido." He was also our Spanish teacher.

By Christmas, Tamy was gone. She was no longer around to pad me as the only welfare child I knew at Slater Junior High. Sporadically, she would call me from random payphones in this little town called Cazadero for the next few months. Then, I never heard from my little helper-spirit again.

The summer before ninth grade my mom decided she didn't want to be a parent anymore, even though I had two younger siblings that were six and four years old. My mom was a newly divorced, thirty-one year-old, and ready to start her life by drowning her loneliness in dancing and drinking with the girls. I didn't know what I was in trouble for one Friday morning, when I was awakened by her and told to get dressed. I met my mom in the front room, sitting on our dingy, old couch smoking. Just like the day Rita called me and gave me my last chance to tell her about my step dad, Bill.

"I'm taking you to the Dependent Unit. I'm not ready to be a parent." She blew out a puff of smoke, "Go eat and then were going." I walked into the kitchen and quietly made my food, as my brother and sister were already eating. In the past few months, she had already started kicking me out; only to call all my friend's parents just as I arrived at their houses to tell them to send me back home. When I arrived home, I was placed back on restriction and sent to my room.

The idea of the Dependent Unit was mixed with a certain freedom from my mom's bullshit and fear of going into the hands of the courts like Tamy did. The only knowledge I had of what was going to be my new home was of Tamy. I never heard her complain about the DU. The feeling I got from her was that she had fun there and she felt safe. She was more worried about going into foster care and not knowing what kind of family she would end up with than she was about living at the DU. She told me there were counselors there that helped with her homework and that they would take the kids on fieldtrips from time to time to Foster Freeze or to Spring Lake. If she came to school every day well fed and with different clothes on, then anything would be better than constantly being sentenced to my room and ridiculed by the snobs for my knock-off clothing.

On our way to the DU, in my mom's faded gold Buick, we were silent. She was chain smoking again and I was having flashbacks of our trip to Howarth Park. This time though, I wasn't scared. In the parking lot, she started to cry. This did not slow her down though. She parked, put out her cigarette in the little metal pull-out ash tray, and marched straight into the building never once looking back at me. The lobby had a feeling of the county welfare office. There was a long, white counter to the right where a woman was signing in children and answering phones. Chairs lined the walls of windows that surrounded the front on the building to the right. I sat down and peered out of the window at Pythian Road and Juvenile Hall.

Its towering, cement walls seemed massive from my new view point. Driving on the highway, the facilities never looked so big—or permanent. From my seat, the fields didn't look like they spanned so far out to the road. The Dependent Unit's play yard was not surrounded by cement like Juvenile Hall, but by little chain link fences. I knew that I could escape, if this place was bad. As my mom filled out a stack of paperwork, she fumbled in her purse for identification cards and information, looking down the whole time, not memorizing any last looks from her eldest daughter. When she was done, she turned in the mound of paperwork. My mother left, crying without an acknowledgement or good-bye, to me.

The woman behind the counter called me up as another woman opened a solid white door behind her and asked if I was next to be processed. Behind the door was a room that was actually a big shower. There were shower heads on the left wall with cabinets and counters on the right side.

"You will need to strip down for a sterile shower and to be checked for lice before I can release you in with the other kids in population. I am going to take your clothes and bag them. They cannot be brought into the center. We have clothes for you here."

I showered in front of her and with her gloves, she probed and processed me. When she was done, she brought me to a room that looked like an enormous coat check. There were clothes everywhere. With cotton shirts and sweats, at first I thought I was in heaven.

"Go ahead. There are undergarments and everything you need to get dressed."

My hair was still wet and my skin was dry from not being able to put any lotion on after my sterile shower. As I rummaged through the clothes, I began to see stains on every item I picked up and holes from extreme wear. A young girl about my age came in, holding a little crippled baby girl with casts on both arms. "She wet herself," she tells the woman. My unconcerned advocate nodded for her to go ahead and change the baby as she left to process the next child.

It was as if these parents were in their grace period with God for their own personal redemption and she had to meet their deadline. The girl saw me fumbling through the mounds of clothes on the floor and the couple of items still barely hanging up.

"Everything has stains on it from the younger girls wearing our sizes and dirtying them. You just have to learn how to hide the stains." She grabbed clothes for the baby and changed her on the clothes strewn on the floor, while I found my new clothes to wear.

"Now what do we do?" I asked as I followed her into a central multi-purpose room in the middle of the building. The room was circular with doors scattered around its parameter. There were younger children sitting at long tables doing projects like coloring, cutting, and pasting. "We play or help out with the younger kids until lunch. This is indoor time. We can go out later," she directs me to the far corner of the room where blankets and pillows are protecting babies on the floor. There were boys watching TV and others playing with an older donated video game. There were kids everywhere and not many counselors I could see or hear.

"What do you mean inside time? And when is lunch?" I ask nervously, sensing my escape plan was being compromised. I sat with her on the floor where a few other girls were playing with the babies that had patches over their eyes or bruises and burn marks visibly apparent on their little bodies. The other girls smiled at me welcoming me into their modest little circle, "We are locked inside until lunch. Even the kitchen is locked and is only open during meal times, so you better eat when they serve you."

Their game strategies flew at me like opening day tryouts. I didn't collect names because that wasn't important. From all the girls, advice was thrown at me. I don't know who was saying what, but I was catching their advice the best way I could with no glove . . . just my bare hands. Their faces were warm and genuine like Tamy's was almost a year earlier. I tried to slip in as many questions between their pitches. They were so good at introducing new kids to the system and all my questions were being answered as soon as I asked them—or well before.

"What if I get hungry in between mealtimes?"

"You don't, they feed us well." One girl said as another finished for her, "and they take us on field trips. Tonight we are going to a baseball game that the teenagers are playing in." A third girl spouts out, "We eat at the games, too. You won't starve here."

"You mean we can play sports?" My running away idea is slowly floating away out the windows that are sealed shut.

"Yeah, the county has teams for us to play on," says someone. I don't know who.

As I was getting my briefing, a baby boy climbed on me and drank his bottle in my lap.

"Where do these babies come from?" As I looked down and saw his dried mucous on his cheek and nose. A Kleenex box appeared in front of my face by a hand in the crowd. "He has sinus infections a lot," says the girl offering the tissues. "He hasn't been here long. The babies are the first to go to foster care or be adopted. As long as they are by themselves . . . with no siblings."

"You mean people just give up their babies?" I asked in the midst of the endless chatter and teething toys tossed through our little field of pillows and blankets.

All the girls piped in, "Oh yeah! Absolutely. All the time. Especially if there are no siblings!" They said in unison, laughing, giggling, and moving on to their next subject.

"What if they have siblings?" Losing my words, I asked them.

"Then CPS tries to keep them together, and they usually stay here longer and eventually get fostered out," the girl sitting next to me said.

One of the counselors, who I hadn't seen sitting at one of the project tables, announced clean-up for lunch. This caused a complete upheaval of younger children running around, putting away coloring books and crayons in bins and older boys and girls picking up games, toys, blankets and pillows and putting them in buckets. Everyone knew what to do and they were doing it without any disciplinary actions called down on them from a random counselor, who was also helping out in the clean-up. By the time the room was in order, the door to the kitchen opened up and, like the girls said, plenty of food was served. More than I had ever eaten at lunch at my mom's house!

They had sandwiches, macaroni and cheese, mashed potatoes, fruit salad, graham crackers, milk, orange juice, apple juice, everything. The kitchen was set up like our junior high school's cafeteria. The older kids helped the younger kids eat. I didn't see any complaining either. Everything was smooth and systematic. No child was left unattended.

The inside counselors were nice, as they appeared to linger in the shadows without much presence for disciplinary supervision. All the kids stayed in their flow and followed along with the crowd in their new-found safe haven away from whatever brought them there in the first place. The alternatives were Juvenile Hall, an abusive home with a dysfunctional family, foster care where a child didn't know if they were going to be abused again, or the Dependent Unit, where we were safely locked up away from the rest of the world.

When we were done, I was led to the back yard lined with fields that led to the freeway. The whole time I was out there playing volleyball, sitting in the shade with the babies in the sand box, or watching the other kids play baseball, I never once thought about escaping. The counselors didn't seem too worried about it, either.

The afternoon went by fast, out in the backyard. Dinner came with another huge meal and following the meal the buses arrived to take us to the game. All of us girls went into the huge closet for sweatshirts and warmer clothes for the younger ones and the babies stayed back at the center with a couple of the counselors. We all piled into the buses and stayed out until dark watching the older teens play in their league. The younger kids climbed through bleachers while the older kids watched with the safe freedom that was felt in the warm Sonoma County evening. The sun went down, leaving the sky in shades of warm pink and lavender. The faint breeze brought in from Bodega cooled off the night quickly in the county and the smell of eucalyptus and sunscreen lingered over the sweaty kids that played outdoors all day.

By the time we got back to the DU, the babies were sound asleep in their nursery. The older girls showed me the girls' wing where we showered and got ready for bed. I was shown to my room, where they would lock me in when it was time to turn the lights off. My room wasn't too small. It had a twin bed in it. Nothing else. The room was rectangle with a large window that did not open. The door had a small double paned window that was too high for me to look through. I was told that if I had to go to the bathroom in the middle of the night that I had to knock on my door and a counselor would let me out to go.

When everyone was done, an announcement was made for us to go into our rooms for lights out. When I got into my bed I heard a solid steel click to my door. Out of my nervousness, I got out of bed and checked my door. A counselor was checking all the doors in the hall by rattling the doors which scared me back into my bed before any arms from under it could grab me. The whole night I thought about that door. I wanted out; to where I didn't know, because I didn't have a place to go. After about an hour, I knocked on my door to use the restroom. The counselor that had locked me in came and let me out.

"The first night is the hardest. It's hard I know, but you're safe and these are our rules. Your mom has called and checked on you, though. I think she is going to come get you soon."

Oh no! My freedom was going to end. This was the closest to summer camp that I would ever get. And, other than being locked in a room at night, I had no other worries in my life, for once, and I had all the food I could possibly eat. I went to the bathroom, got a reassuring smile on my return, and was locked back into my room again with that crushing deep metal sound as my door lock ground into its chamber. This time when I walked back to my bed I wasn't worried about any monsters underneath it. After a while of looking out of my bedroom window and seeing the far off lights of the speeding cars from the highway, I fell soundly asleep in my little 'cell'.

The morning came with a loud click from the doors in our hall. A counselor that I hadn't seen before opened our doors, chiming "Rise and shine girls." I saw a couple of girls come out of their rooms and go into the bathroom. Some came into my room to see how I slept my first night, "How was it?"

"It's not that big of a deal, huh?"

"I remember my first night."

"Yeah, and you blubbered and said you had to go the bathroom at least ten times. You woke us all up," random questions and chatter again came flying at me.

"We are not supposed to be in each other's rooms, so get dressed and come to breakfast."

One-by-one they drifted out and dispersed between our coat check closet and the bathroom to brush their teeth and wash up. The next two days were filled with activities in the great room; playtime with the younger kids; and kickball outdoors. A counselor pulled me aside after breakfast on Sunday and told me my mom was coming to get me. I asked her if she was allowed to do that and she said she was because there was no record of abuse by her.

"You know, you're one of the lucky ones. A lot of these kids are left here and are put into the system. Your mom has called numerous times these past three days. She will figure it out. You'll be fine. You're in counseling right? " she said assuredly more to herself than me. I came into the DU without any bruises and my abuser according to CPS was out of the house. At this point, I was the least of their worries. My mom's tantrum was realized and the county had kids of greater need to worry about.

After lunch that day my mom came and got me. I was given my old clothes to change back into and my mother met me in the lobby. She was crying, but not looking at me, and I was aggravated that my summer camp was over. In the Buick on our way home, no questions were asked and no apologies were made. By the time we got home, and a couple cigarettes later, I was given a list of chores to do. For whatever reason, I was back on restriction just like before I left for my 'summer vacation'. My life went right back to the way it was before I left. My mom never said why she sent me away that weekend or even once asked what happened to me while I was there.

WINDOW HOPPING

How does it feel to treat me like you do?
When you've your hands upon me
And told me who you are
I thought I was mistaken
I thought I heard your words
Tell me, how do I feel
Tell me now, How do I feel
Those who came before me
Lived through their vocations
From the past until completion
They'll turn away no more
And I still find it so hard
To say what I need to say
But I'm quite sure that you'll tell me
Just how I should feel today

"Blue Monday" by New Order

One afternoon, a friend from school and work at Little Ceasars, and I decided to make Fuzzy Navels and drink them in the gorgeous midday sun overlooking the beautiful scenery near her house. Despite the fact that we were under age, it was extremely easy to get our hands on the alcohol from a patron out in front of the grocery store. Using 'Big Gulp' cups, our tonics were concocted sparing the ice, as we lay out in the sun, drinking, giggling and paying no attention to any consequences we would face if we got caught.

At some point we went into her room to listen to music and basically passed out. Around dinner time, my friend's mother had come home. Not noticing our intoxication, she woke me up for a phone call from my mother.

"Come home for dinner," She directed. Before she hung up, I lied, telling her I had already eaten. "Then come home to do the dishes," she hung up.

Thinking that I was sober, I woke up my friend, Denise, and asked her to drive me home. Once I started up my mom's porch, I realized that I needed to hold myself together. Denise recognized it too and helped me up the steps. My mom was sitting in her living room watching TV when I went straight to the kitchen to wash the dishes, intending to go straight to my room as soon as I was finished. There I could pass out. Denise stayed to help me clean up the kitchen as I was apparently not anywhere near sober. In fact, I had trouble staying upright while trying to keep the dish water in the sink.

My mother caught on to the commotion rather quickly, ordering Denise to leave. Striking my head with her fists and grabbing me by the hair, she pulled me into the bedroom. Denise dodged her as best she could while I tried to catch my footing, screaming for her to let me go. Desperately, I grabbed at her hands to save my scalp from her tightening grip. Denise ran out the front and around my house to my bedroom window. She watched as my mother kept lifting me up against the wall punching and grabbing at me. She tried to make me stand upright for a fair fight, only to have me collapse with each blow. My screaming and crying kept Denise glued to the window, until a final blow knocked me out onto my bed. Terrified to be seen, and completely sober by now, Denise crept out of my backyard, hiding from my mom, and scrambling home.

The next day I woke up to my mom's new friend, Jerry, who was now staying with us, stroking my head. Not fully awake, I started to throw up as he rushed me to the bathroom. Dazed and confused as to how long I slept or what had happened, I looked in the mirror to find my head swollen and bruised.

"Your mom is pretty mad at you. You came home drunk and tried to clean the kitchen but you couldn't even stand up without your friend helping you." He handed me a rag for my face.

"I don't remember seeing you." I fell back onto the cold bathtub wall.

"No. I wasn't here. When I came home you were already passed out. You got up a few times to throw up, and I guess that's how you hit your head. I don't know," as he shook his head. "But she's pissed. She said if you wake up before she gets home to pack your stuff and leave. It's not good." He shook his head, leaving the bathroom.

I got up from the floor, my head still pounding and took a long shower. My head was throbbing as I called a friend to pick me up. When I got someone to come get me, I took some aspirin and went into my room to start packing. It was a blessing that my ride came before my mom's arrival. After a couple nights at a friend's house, I got a ride to Mom's older brother's house.

My uncle Mike was a bar manager at a high-end restaurant in Walnut Creek. He was very good looking and 'very' single. Even when he had a girlfriend, he was *very* single. My mom's two older brothers and my nanu were the only men in my life that I looked up to and felt safe with. They had kept a distance from my mom's shenanigans, yet loved her and me with a protective eye.

"Chris, you're my favorite. I'd do anything for you, but you can't live with me." Uncle Mike obstinately shook his head, got up from his bed, and leaned against his black and gold oversized 80s retro wood dresser.

His arms stretched out, his long fingers gripped his matching egg shaped footboard. I sat on his bed, crying. At 15 years old, my mother kicked me out for the last time and I began to realize that my mother's escape-from-her-own-reality-shenanigans would always haunt me. I thought I was pretty convincing in my proposal, pointing out that I would get a job at night and go to school during the day. I only had two more years of high school. He would never see me and I would sleep on his couch. I would preserve his bachelorhood. This was a solid case on my behalf.

"No, I can't save your mom again. She has to figure this out." He paced, shook his head some more, and meandered back and forth through his narrow path around his big furniture.

"Nanu and Nana told her to get her act together or they would take you from her. If she didn't come get you, they were going to take you. But, she kept running away or tried to off herself. No, she has to take responsibility for her actions. You know she tried to give you up, but it didn't work, don't you? The doctor messed up somehow." He rambled as he paced.

"Lack of . . . she's careless; always has been with you. Look at you, look at the others . . . and Bill, that scumbag. She can't just give up on you and kick you out when she doesn't get what she wants. She's spoiled. You can visit and stay when you need to but you can't live here. My life is set. I can't have a teenager in my condo. The bar is too much, nuh-huh. No Chris, I can't."

He picked up his pack of Benson & Hedges and walked out to his balcony table with his Amstel Light. I went into his kitchen, grabbed his mother's frosted raisin cookies and a Pepsi, and sat facing him on his little patio table. My begging tear-stained face watched him as he smiled at his groupies down at the pool. They all smiled and waved up at us. He gave his two-finger salute wave, inhaled, and half-assed chuckled.

"But, I have nowhere to go, Uncle Mike. Uncle Mike."

He looked at me and blew smoke from the side of mouth. Then he put his cigarette down and grabbed my hands.

"You stay this weekend and figure it out. I'll call your mom, but you can't stay here. This is her responsibility. She's been pawning you off all your life. You and the kids are her responsibility. She did this when you were young. I remember. I was there."

My saving grace was that some of my friends had their driver's licenses. I convinced Uncle Mike to feed one of them if she came to pick me up from his condo in Concord that Sunday night.

That following Monday I went back to climbing into windows at night, crawling into beds for warmth, and burying my head deep into the blankets and bodies of my friends. I begged God to take away the throbbing surges of fire that captured my medulla oblongata[2] and strangled my brain guts from all my crying. I snuck showers in the mornings before school, borrowed clothes, scrubbed my underwear with the bathroom's Ivory soap, blew them dry while I dried my hair, and scarffed down whatever extra breakfast could be smuggled for me. This was all mastered as I jumped back out of the window, ran down the street, and waited for the same friend's parents to pick me up on the corner for a ride to school.

Sometimes I would be allowed to stay at a friend's house for a sporadic week here or there. I avoided one friend's house. Her bedroom door had been removed so that her father could have access to her anytime he wanted. Another friend eventually ran away with her uncle because he was her coke supplier. If my friends were to get into any sort of trouble though during my stay, I would be the first privilege they would lose.

---

[2] The medulla oblongata is the lower half of the brainstem.

One wealthy family made me call my mom to get approval to stay at their house. That resulted in my first altercation with the Santa Rosa Police Department where I filed for emancipation, which she later signed off on. She had called the police one night to bring me home from my job. When they arrived at my work, I tried to run out the back door. I ran right into the hefty arms of my overweight boss, Rich, who carried me back up to the front and into the waiting cops' hands. Being hand cuffed in a police car, as my mom waited for us at the station, got me pretty ticked off. When she tried to pronounce me a 'runaway,' I corrected her.

As my words tumbled over each other and ricocheted off the white wall of the familiar interrogation room, she quickly realized it would be in her best interest to sign my papers. She had no interest in answering to the authorities about her lack of child rearing and safety for me.

The one good thing about staying with the wealthy family was establishing a system of handing my paychecks to the mom, who started a savings account for me. She informed me once "Children should not live outside their parents' homes. It is just unnatural." She didn't like the liability, yet she saved my money for me and I eventually grew on her. At one point, she let me buy a dress and shoes for a turnabout that year.

Another family was as dysfunctional as mine. My friend's single mother was an avid pot smoker. She caught me climbing in the window one time, told me my friend wasn't home, and to go to bed. Our jobs as teenagers, under her apartment roof, were to keep our room clean and keep her well supplied with weed. If not, it was a scream fest. Things like not putting the toilet paper on the right way, or not putting our hand-washed underwear away, or not having enough quarters for the washing machine all set her off on a rage. This scared me away from that house.

It quickly became a pattern of mine to sleep in any available bed I could find, which meant this mother never knew where I was. She forced my friend to call and look for me so I could come back to her home and clean.

One house I stayed at included a group of newly graduated friends that had gone to Montgomery or Santa Rosa High. There were six of us in a tiny three bedroom apartment. I slept in a bed when it was available. There was a lot of sleeping on the floor and sharing of beds.

On school nights, I would be awakened by some random straggler from a party in the front room who thought it was cute that I had school in the morning. They offered me a drink and wanted to climb into bed with me because they were ready to pass out. In the morning, whoever was my cuddling buddy or passed out on the front room floor was my ride to school. I always had a ride.

With my work permit, I landed my first job at Little Caesar's Pizza in Bennett Valley. My dinners came from here, later from Mary's Pizza Shack, and then wherever else I could get hired. Eating buns from the bread warmer sometimes was my highlight meal of the day. I hid in the bathroom, swallowing as fast as I could before any attention was drawn that I was missing. One job I landed was at a bagel shop that opened at six in the morning. The bagels were made in the main shop downtown, so someone needed to be at my shop by five to load all the display baskets and fill all the spreads. I was able to accomplish my opening chores and be relieved by the time the first bell rang at school.

At one point, I had three part-time jobs and maintained my school attendance. My paychecks were small and I tried to contribute as best as I could where ever I was living, barely having enough to cover food on a regular daily basis. I borrowed my friend's clothes, folded and tucked to make them fit, and gladly wore whatever was donated for the day.

Graduating from high school was a feat I am amazed I accomplished. School quickly became a catch up race with all my assignments, barely passing every class by mere points. In order for me to graduate, I had 54 absences that needed to be accounted for. Being an emancipated minor, it allowed me to write my notes for justifying my court dates (for driving without a license), my absences for work, or my random irresponsibility.

Being pulled over became a regular pastime, and not having a license racked up a regular schedule of court dates. My accident didn't help my case and neither did getting caught driving down one way streets in San Francisco.

Darren and I have been friends since the seventh grade. We go to shows almost every weekend together. Still to this day, he will not get his license due to the trauma caused by my inexperience of the California driving laws.

I was able to barely walk on Graduation Day with my fellow classmates, by the grace of God.

THE BANANA SPLIT

We're just two lost souls
Swimming in a fish bowl,
Year after year,
Running over the same old ground.
And how we found
The same old fears.

"Wish You Were Here" by Pink Floyd

In the pouring rain, I am having a hard time seeing anything in front of me through my windshield. Dry and cracked, my windshield wipers aren't making much of a difference, either. My little Datsun B-210 is trying really hard to keep up with the rest of the cars on Highway 12. The highway, to this day still doesn't have any lights. After years of driving it, most of us have memorized the road and all its curves.

Highway 12, a two lane highway with free grave sites plotted along its sidelines, is strewn with hand-made crosses and fake flowers tied to trees. The highway from Santa Rosa to Sonoma has a couple of straight-a-ways where locals speed up in order to get through the long drive quicker. Since it is such a popular tourist area, the road gets sprinkled with people that like to cruise and enjoy the scenery no matter what time of day it is. They also don't know the road or where the deer or other animals tend to bound out.

Just before you enter Sonoma, and before you pass through
Agua Caliente, on the left hand side is a giant tree stump. People
stop to take pictures of it. It's that huge! Years ago the tree fell
over and was uprooted, with its roots fanning out along the side
of the highway reaching over ten feet tall and wide. The tree
itself was cut away after it fell and the roots were left as sort of
an art structure to compliment the beautiful landscape of the
Sonoma County vineyards.

Directly across the road from the stump is BR Cohn
Wineries, a wooden fence with just a few planks, and thick
round posts encompassing numerous rows of grapes. Fences for
the various vineyards aren't set too far back from the road, so
tourists can pose for scenic shots and take close ups of the
grapes. Apparently one row of grapes is worth a lot of money.

Hood House is playing in Sonoma and my car, which
legally seats four, has six teenagers in it . . . Mary, Travis, Tony,
Ritchie, Darren, and myself. I am the only one that has a
working seat belt. Mary is sitting on Travis's lap in the
passenger seat and in the back are Tony, Darren, and Ritchie.
Until recently, Darren and I had been hitching rides with
whoever had their license, to get to the weekend shows. Now
that I have my car, Darren and I are hitting every show we hear
about.

Tonight, I still do not have my license and Darren has been
there to share in my experience of accepting my first two tickets.
Tony is a younger neighbor and Mary is a friend I have recently
become close with as we have in common the unwanted high
school homelessness experience. She had been staying at Selena

Tucker's, an elementary school girlfriend. I met Travis tonight for the first time; he is friends with Mary and Tony. Ritchie is my boyfriend's little brother. Ritchie and Darren have become pretty close the past couple of months and Ritchie is now our little junior high tag-a-long.

Earlier tonight, I told my mom that my car was getting an oil change and was being left over night until I could pick it up in the morning. A week before, she found out about my prior tickets and thought I should park my car until I could legally drive. I partly thought she was right. That's why I lied to her about the work being done on it tonight. By this time in my life she really didn't have much control over me and I came and went as I pleased. I only moved back to her house a couple months prior so I could graduate from high school.

My music is blasting the mixed tape of local funk and punk music from the bands we are about to see. Everyone is talking all at once. There is broken singing in and out of conversation, a complete ADD fest. The three boys in the back are getting high and listening to their own Walkmans. I am yelling at them to roll down the one window that works. They complain about the rain and the possibility of getting wet if they do. Mary and Travis are my co-pilots. We are following Mary's friend, Tamara.

Tamara's car is newer than my Datsun, a.k.a. the banana, and she is going much faster than our Flintstone feet can take us. My car is a true beater in every possible sense and a perfect first car for someone who will wreck it within six months of ownership. It is very square and bright yellow. When the motor is on, it has that puttering sound as if it is a diesel. It is, in fact, a clutch with one of those long metal stick shifts. Whenever I go over the slightest bump, the whole car rattles and the passengers in the back seat fly up and hit their heads on the ceiling. I enjoy doing this to the boys. The Datsun doesn't have a thick dashboard, so Mary's long legs have plenty of room.

All of a sudden, Darren looks down at my dimly lit console and says, "Christina, I think you should slow down!"

"We're going to lose Tamara" Mary interrupts and then goes back to talking to Travis.

"Do you know how to get there?" I interrupt, speaking to anyone in the car. I don't hear an answer. I look down and notice the thin metal needle through the scratched plastic cover stagger close to sixty. I press on my brakes and we watch the lights of Tamara's car in front of us get smaller as they fade through the sheets of rain.

The rain is beating down hard on us and I am coming up on the turn with the massive tree stump. So I slam down even more on my brakes . . .

A sense of floating comes over our now gliding shelter from the rain storm outside, and it feels like the banana is building momentum. The back of my car starts to skid sideways, back and forth, side to side. I don't know what is happening. I struggle with the steering wheel to stay straight, and to move forward. My foot slams my brake pedal down even further to the disintegrating frayed carpet and the slippery metal floor. By now, my legs have become lifeless and they are not on the pedals anymore. I am in absolute silence. I can't hear anyone or anything in the car. I am heading straight for the tree stump, so I pull the steering to the right tightly.

The banana catches flight.

I close my eyes into complete darkness. I hear again. It's everyone bumping around in the car, flying and bouncing off each other. There are grunts and the sound of glass crushing, like little puzzle pieces or squares flying throughout the car as if they were popcorn cooking in the Jiffy Pop dome.

My door flies off, my seat belt keeps bringing me back to my seat, and yet I feel the left side of my face scrape against something. My eyes are still locked shut. My face is getting colder and wetter. An enormous weight and force is whipping all of us with its powerful whirl.

I wake up to everyone yelling at me, "Christina! Christina, wake up! Shit, she's got to wake up!" and tugging at my seat belt. I open my eyes and see my headlights shining on grapevines and wire through the pouring rain. There's darkness from my upside down view. The boys release my seatbelt and I fall with a loud thump. I hear the sound of my hair ripping out of my scalp and feel numb to any pain in my body. After the boys get me free they all scatter. Wandering off like zombies, not one of them is looking back at me. They are completely oblivious, following their own agenda.

I fall on someone and kick off of their stomach taking the air out of them to climb out of the front passenger window.

Mary wakes up and screams for me to come back to help her get out. Her head is stuck and she can't move from inside of the car. I turn around in a daze and climb back over the slippery, mud washed, beat up twisted metal. My legs stick straight up in the air, keeping me from falling back in. I see the black and white pig on wheels Christmas ornament still hanging from the mangled rearview mirror. The only way I can think to get her out, is to yank on her arms. Her hair is pinned under a large wooden pole used to hold up grape vines. It has shot through her window and secured our landing spot and Mary's head. Now, what I know my hair was stuck on.

A huge amount of hair rips out of Mary's head when I finally get her free. She doesn't scream and shows no sign of pain either. She manages to kick off something inside and climbs out of the car with me. We slide off the car as everyone talks independently, going in all different directions.

I hear Darren tell Ritchie they have to bury his pipe and their weed. I see Travis limping up to the side of the road and groaning. Tony is on the road trying to stop traffic with his bare hands. I hear the slap of his hands bouncing off of cars as they speed by us. Brilliant sparks haphazardly shoot out from the highway through the heavy rain and then darkness as each speeding car flicks off of lingering metal from the banana. A drowned out clank, as the metal torpedoes in different directions off each side of the road, follows.

I turn to Mary, "Let's just lock up my car and turn off my lights so my battery doesn't go dead and walk to Hood House."

"Alright," she endorses. We both turn towards the vineyard and start screaming to Darren and Ritchie, "You guys, get the keys and turn the lights off in the car. Let's go, we can still make it! Come on guys!" They don't turn to acknowledge us nor do we wait to get it. They are still out in the vineyard. Mary turns to me, "Tamara must have seen us. I'm sure she's pulled off up there. Let's just go in her car." I agree as we struggle up the slippery wet slope to the road and proceed to walk to Agua Caliente in the rain.

We are completely soaked. Our hair is matted and standing straight up in the air despite the rain pouring down on us. I only have one shoe on, limping. The left side of my face is filled with dirt, rubble, and blood. I can feel with every step, the sloshing of water and mud between my toes, water burbling out with each step out of the top patent leather penny loafers.

Mary is confident we will see Tamara's car at any moment pulled over waiting for us to jump in. With each passing car, she asks, "Is that her? Come on let's check. No that's her. Hurry, come on. No, that's her." I hobble behind, anxious to just get in the girl's car. Neither of us is concerned with what just happened. We don't look back. In fact, our only thoughts are to get to the concert. The realization of the enormity of damage that has just occurred is not in our spectrum of thought or knowingness at this time.

A little ways up the road, a car pulls over, a man leans out, and rolls down his window, "You girls were in an accident down the road and you have to come back. The ambulance is on its way."

"I don't need an ambulance," I insist. "I'm fine. I locked up my car and I'm going to come back to it in the morning." We haven't stopped walking. Mary is too busy looking for Tamara's car. The guy slowly follows alongside of us and we act like he isn't there, blabbing about if we are going to miss the show, who's opening for them, and agreeing that we will definitely have a ride home once we get there. Mary stops suddenly and turns to our stalker, "We are going to walk to our show. We are fine . . . the guys are coming." I hobble up next to her and shake my head in agreement.

The man bargains with us, "Look, you have to come back and tell the ambulance you don't want to go with them. Your friends are going to go with them but you have to tell them. Then you can go to your show. Okay?"

We linger and ponder. After a few minutes of deep deliberation about missing Tamara and maybe the show, we climb into this man's car. We continue to devise and strategize plan B to get to our destination and for the first time, we notice each other's hair. We are both sitting in the passenger seat fixing each other's hair, pulling twigs out, and flattening our tangled beehives the best we can so that when we get to the show we'll still look stunning.; I think.

He makes a u-turn but we don't acknowledge him. He pulls up to where the boys are, we get out still fussing with each other, and again we don't acknowledge him. The man drives off, I think. We don't look back to thank him. We are so bugged by this set-back he has just created for us.

I get out of the car and Tony runs up to me screaming, hands cupped around his nose, "Christina, my nose!" His nose is a flap of skin hanging on the side of his face and his hands are covered with blood. I look at him and at this point still don't totally register what is going on. He doesn't wait for a response from either of us and goes back to trying to stop cars with his hands. The ambulance hasn't shown up yet. Travis is just sitting there on the side of the road groaning about his leg. As we walk towards him, Darren and Ritchie come over the hill. Glass shards are sticking out of their scalps which are oozing blood like fake Halloween costume accessories. We all just stare at Tony in silence and I look back and see that my car lights are still on.

I start yelling, "Darren, I told you to turn off the lights and get my keys! I don't have my license. I can't go in the ambulance." Darren and Ritchie don't say a word to me. They just head back down to the car to accommodate me and shut me up. Both shake their heads in bewilderment.

A few minutes later the ambulance pulls up and at first, none of us have any interest in dealing with the two paramedics. I immediately yell out as loudly as I can, "I'm not going with you guys. I'm fine! My car is locked up. I'm going to come back in the morning for it," I exclaim as I turn from them and start walking down the road again with Mary.

Darren and Ritchie head back from getting my keys and are veering towards Agua Caliente. They follow us when they see the paramedics acting like officers from the Humane Society who have been called out to corral a bunch of wounded, disorientated animals. Their arms are out to their sides ready to tackle and restrain at any moment.

One paramedic targets and pounces on Ritchie, noticing his silver medical bracelet. Ritchie twists and wiggles his arm out of his grip, while the paramedic is trying to read his bracelet.

"You guys wait up. Don't leave me. I want to go with them," Ritchie begs us to wait.

"Yeah, I don't think so. You're a diabetic." The paramedic finally gets a hold of his bracelet. "You're coming with us. Oh, shit! You're Dick Michaelsen's son."

The other paramedic looks up at this announcement and goes back to his task of getting Tony off the freeway. Eventually, Ritchie gives in from exhaustion, and climbs into his stretcher in the ambulance. Tony is screaming, "My nose! Look at my nose!" running up and down the freeway frantically.

The second paramedic is trying to get him to focus so he will realize they are here to help him. "Son. Son. Calm down. I can help you," as he weaves back and forth, trying to get Tony to stop for a minute, "You have to come with me. Son. Son!"

Finally Tony slows down and fixates on him, "My nose. Look at my nose!"

"I know. I know," arms out, trying to catch him. "You have to come with me." He lures him like he has a carrot tied to a string.

By now we are back down the street with Darren, who is smoking. Bloody glass is sticking out of his head. Travis is next because he can't walk anyway. He just sits there moaning, on the side of the road. He is in so much pain that he just doesn't care. With the paramedic's help he limps to his spot in the white van with the big red lights beating through all the rain.

We hear someone run up from behind. Mary and I refuse to turn and look at him. Darren now floats along with us calmly as my shoe squirts out water with every other step I take. As the paramedic walks alongside our awkward stumbling, he tells us we HAVE to go with him. I stop. "I can't go with you. I don't have medical insurance or a license. I want to come back tomorrow and get my car." I plead with him to leave me alone.

"The Highway Patrol is at your car now. You have to come back. You won't get in trouble if you come with us. Your friends need help and you do, too." Darren and Mary stop walking and head back. We see the police directing traffic now and what's strange is that they are not looking for me or trying to talk to me. Mary asks him if we can still make the show, as if he personally going to drive us there.

"If you hurry, maybe," his impatience is brewing. We all look at each other, Darren follows our lead. More deliberation occurs, our backs are turned from our insistent catcher of people—not dogs—we whisper with each other, and start to walk towards the ambulance very quietly.

As we walk back, I don't get approached by any of the officers. They don't come to talk to me. They direct traffic, they look in the vineyard, they talk to the tow truck driver, they try to figure out how anyone survived, and they discuss how they are going to get the mangled banana out of the third row of the vineyard.

I feel like I am invisible to them. It seems like they are so far away, yet they are just a few feet from me, moving in slow motion. I am not able to hear what they are saying, but I can see their mouths moving, organizing, and strategizing how to clean up this mess I am leaving them with.

When we get to the door of the ambulance, in all its brightness, I can see everyone. . . .

Ritchie is on a stretcher with a plastic mask over his nose and a big white neck brace. His eyes are closed. Tony has his head back, with white rags or towels tie-dyed red covering his face and now he is quiet. Travis and Darren are sitting on the side benches, looking like they visited hell and barely got out alive. Mary and I climb in last; the white in the rainy darkness finally jolts me into the severity of what is rapidly unfolding in front of me.

My heart starts to feel heavy from my careless annihilation of the night. The paramedic gives me a cold pack and tells me to hold it lightly against my face. I start weeping. Mary starts bawling. The boys are all sedated, comatose, and quiet. The siren is loud and the only other sound is Mary and me blubbering. The pain starts, the excruciating pain in my face, my left hand, and my left ankle. Mary complains of a headache and her hair is matted and full of blood. No one else is talking. The paramedic in the back tends to all of us quietly. My tears are burning my face and every time I try to touch it rubble falls into my lap.

When we pull up to the hospital we are greeted by tons of nurses and people I don't know who they are or what they do. Someone helps me out of the ambulance and directs me to follow the crowd. A couple of steps away, I hear, "Hey, how is she walking?" I turn around to see two men pointing to my left ankle. I look down and see a piece of metal sticking out of my left ankle with a thin steady stream of blood filling my shoe, mixing with the muddy water gushing through my toes. I look down and it starts to hurt. He asks me if I need help walking in and I shake my head no, then turn and limp into the hospital through the double doors where I am greeted with a nurse that brings me to a phone to call my mom.

There is a rustling "Hello?"

"Ma, I got in an accident going to Sonoma."

"How? Who was driving?"

"Me"

"What car?"

"Mine"

"How did you get it?"

"I went back and took it."

"Were you drinking?"

"No"

Silence . . .

"Are you ok?"

"I don't know"

"Where are you?"

I ask the nurse where I am and she tells me to go lay down. She takes the phone from me.

I wake up to my mom crying and a doctor picking rubble out my face with long thin metal tweezers. He tells my mom that each day I will have to soak off the ointment he is giving me with a warm rag and put on fresh medicine. "She is going to need stitches in her hand and ankle but not on her face. I can use a butterfly on her chin, though. I can't believe any of these kids made it."

My mom starts bawling. That makes me cry, the tears burning my left cheek. The doctor tries to swab my face with that white gauze stuff and tells me to try to stop crying.

A nurse tells my mom that it will be okay and to collect herself. She tells her that her crying is not helping the doctor get through all the crap imbedded in my face.

My door flew open in the accident and I was the only one with a seat belt on. In our flips, I was lifted out of my seat and my face scrapped against the ground outside. The entire left side of my face is scraped raw, engrained with dirt. There is a deep laceration on my chin. I see Ritchie's mom and dad come in to see me, dressed elegantly from an event. His dad is a political official in our community, the Sherriff of Sonoma County. I am guessing this will not be good press for him. When the ambulance driver saw Ritchie's name, his dad was dispatched right away.

They heard about the details of our wreck over the radio on their drive to Sonoma. Ritchie's dad says in his calm political voice, "Everything is going to be okay. They were just concerned about Ritchie's insulin level, that's all," as he is gently patting my arm, his hand trembling on his own. "He and Darren just got cleaned up, heads shaved with stitches. The girl just has bruises. Travis has a broken leg."

Ritchie's mom interrupts, "Sweetie, no one is mad at you. All the parents are here. You are okay. It's okay." She is reassuring me, rubbing my same arm.

"What about Tony?" I whimper.

"Oh, he's going to be fine. They are taking him to Memorial as they don't have the resources here to do his surgery. He'll be fine."

After my doctor is done plucking at my face and putting a butterfly on the deep gash on my chin, which seems to take forever, he slathers me with a gelatinous ointment that congeals as it sits on my cheek. From the corner of my eye, I can see creamy little mountain ranges with little peaks like the tops of meringue pies or like the snowy Alps you see in pictures at a great distance.

I have never seen stitches performed on anyone before nor have I been a patient in a hospital. When the doctor walks up with a needle and black thread, I'm in awe how primitive it is. I'm in this hospital with all these big machines flashing numbers with lines arching up and down in rhythms, pulsing and chirping out a beep every exact moment. My doctor tells me I'm going to feel a little tug and that it won't hurt too badly. My eyes widen in disbelief. I'm speechless. I don't believe that he really is going to sew me like I have seen my nana do millions of times on our clothes.

If he is serious, then I would rather her do it as I trust her a lot more when it comes to sewing something seamlessly. I look around at the adults and no one is stopping him. Darren comes in with his freak show magnet radar, ready for his gory demo. All he is missing is his popcorn, "Christina, look! I got mine already," he bends down to show me his shaved spots on his head and the little perfect knots of black string sticking out like little alien radars with their heads hiding in his scalp. "Ritchie has his, too." I ignore his pep talk and ask where Ritchie is and his dad says that he is still in his bed being monitored.

Ritchie's parents give me kisses and his mother whispers in my ear that no one is mad at me one more time and that everything will be taken care of. "Just you watch, trust me," as they leave to go back to check on Ritchie.

Darren is known for having crazy contraptions on such "you won't believe it unless you see it" occasions and he is upset with himself that he doesn't have some type of filming device to record this gruesome episode of me. My mom and the other parents are used to ignoring Darren and tell my doctor he won't go away, so it would be best to continue.

As the doctor tugs and pokes at me, my mom tells me to look at her as she asks me questions about the accident. I am unable to really help her. Darren has become my new nurse, with twigs still sticking out of his head. I feel the thread sliding through my skin, a sensational pull as real to me as almost killing all six of us.

Afterwards in the lobby and in the morning when everyone is back together again, my friends are surprisingly sympathetic. I continue to lose it when I see all their wounds, the accident sight, and the flat s shaped banana. As a team, we filter through the metal that barely resembles a vehicle anymore and through the vineyard and take out whatever belongings we find. We are silent.

A couple of years later, we reunited around another car accident. We were all there . . . Ritchie in spirit. He had been in San Diego for the weekend and was driving home with a friend.

They had just entered Santa Rosa and were on a windy road just like our Highway 12 accident a couple years before. Their car ran off the side of the road and hit a tree much smaller than our monumental sculpture. Ritchie was the passenger and with his diabetes, could not sustain the trauma this time. Our little brother was 17 when we said our goodbyes at his funeral.

CHOICE

We will grieve not, rather find
Strength in what remains behind;
In the primal sympathy
Which having been must ever be;
In the soothing thoughts that spring
Out of human suffering;
In the faith that looks through death,
In years that bring the philosophic mind

Ode on Intimations of Immortality from Recollections of Early
Childhood, William Wordsworth

At some point in my senior year, I went back to my mom's house in order to graduate. This was based on an agreement that the day after I graduated, I would leave and go back to raising myself.

It was in her bathroom that I soiled my little white dipstick and discovered I was pregnant. I was seventeen years old. Renting wasn't an option, even though I was an emancipated minor. Having a child when I was about to be homeless in less than a month, added to my already unstable launch once again from my mother's nest. Learning to fly with a newborn wasn't an option I could fathom.

When I wept out my confession to my mother, her only response was, "You better take care of it, and quick before it's too late."

Her face, stern and as cold as the hallowed piggy bank she made for me when I was younger, showed no mercy in her conviction. Taking me to our family doctor to see about an abortion was her only contribution in the matter. Talking to the doctor, who I had known my whole childhood, didn't instill any assurance of having a choice, either.

The father of my embryo was in full agreement with my mother and my doctor. Fumbling out words, in between choked up sobs, brought forth a confession of what his father thought of me. His suggestion, that my boyfriend find a nice blonde girl who wouldn't end up barefoot and pregnant within the year, was noted.

Considering the father's prediction of me, a baby would have made me a statistic that neither of us wanted to fulfill. Again, a firm vote to not proceed with my pregnancy was asserted. Our relationship was on the newer side and neither of us professed our love to each other or vowed to spend the rest of our growing years together. There were no comforting words of endearment in that conversation, only a promise that I dispose of the fertilized seed within me in a timely manner.

The reactions produced from my announcement created only one numb option. I did not see a life with a child at that time; neither did anyone else I had shared the news with. Acknowledging that a child was in me wasn't registering, either. I knew my doctor performed the procedures in his office, making it safer than going to a clinic or unfamiliar grounds.

Decision making and planning becomes minimal when one is just going through the motions. Most of my energy consisted of salvaging my diploma and working for my meals. My job was bussing tables at Orlando's in downtown Santa Rosa, about two miles away from where my mom lived in the Montgomery Village area. Not very far by car, but walking or using the bike my friend's mom lent to me use was exhausting. Normally, I would get off work after a dinner shift that ended around ten or eleven o'clock at night, arrive home around one in the morning, and then head to school later that same morning.

With all that in mind, my procedure was scheduled for an afternoon. I asked one of my girlfriends to take me, stay with me, and drive me home. The decision makers were nowhere to be found. I met her after school, still emotionless to my task at hand. Asking me if I was okay, she pulled out. Silence fell over me as she chatted about school, grades, and her senior trip at the end of the year.

The doctor's office was just over the hill and her bug climbed it at a snail's pace. The smell of eucalyptus blew in through my window. The crisp spring air filled the car with warmth, yet goose bumps covered my arms and naked legs under my oversized skirt. An uncontrollable trembling started at the root of my abdomen, underneath where my baby rested, and shot straight down to the inside of my knees.

Vigorously rubbing my legs, I tried to generate any form of blood flow. It wasn't working. As she pulled into a parking spot, she smiled a smile of comfort and reassurance that she would stay and wait for me. Convincing my legs to gain control and get their act together while I opened the car door demanded my complete focus. One step at a time.

As the office door opened, the soft ding-ding signaled my arrival. The receptionist looked up, greeted me with a smile, and brought me back to reality.

My friend nudged me forward as she found her seat in the waiting room for the remainder of the afternoon. I didn't have to wait long. The nurse behind the receptionist buzzed me in after I signed their log-in sheet. She welcomed me with an arm around my shoulder, rubbing away all my goose bumps, and squeezing the fear out of me. My procedure room was the same room I had been examined in numerous times before. My vaccinations, my sicknesses, my check-ups were all in that familiar room.

The warmth from the familiarity soothed me, even with the extra apparatus positioned by my bed. After I changed into my smock, my nurse came in to prep me with the sedation. As she comforted me, my doctor walked in, asking me if I was ready. I nodded, wordless. He asked me if my friend was staying to take me home. I nodded as my nurse pricked me and I was out.

I woke up on a couch in an office room. I had never been here. I tried to sit up, only to fall back onto my pillow. My nurse directed me to stay put a little while longer. Dozing off, I awoke to my friend wiping my hair away from my face, gently rousing me. As she shifted for me to sit up, I felt my body fall forward and land on the floor. Her gasp summoned the nurse to help her hoist me back onto the couch, where I stayed for a while against my friend's shoulder. On my second try, I was able to make a wavering stand and with arm-in-arm we made it to my friend's car. I kept my eyes closed and lowered the back of my seat.

When I got home, my friend walked me past my mother and the kids, and helped me to bed, where I stayed until the next morning. Then my day started all over again, with work and school. My condition was rectified per my census and was never discussed again.

RUNNING FASTER THAN MY FEET CAN TAKE ME

But the waitin feel is fine:
So don't treat me like a puppet on a string,
cause I know I have to do my thing.
Don't talk to me as if you think 'I'm dumb;
I wanna know when you're gonna come - soon.
I don't wanna wait in vain for your love;
cause if summer is here,
I'm still waiting there;
Winter is here,
And I'm still waiting there.

"Waiting in Vain" by Bob Marley

For the whole decade of my twenties, I was enrolled in some class or another at the local junior college, working at least two jobs (mostly waiting tables at night and working in retail or at the health club during the day), and burning through relationships. Those usually ended in tantrums fueled with my anger and lack of trust for anybody.

My dating wasn't serious. And I certainly was not contributing to society in any positive manner. To make sure that I really had no time to feel anything, I drank heavily with a group of girlfriends most nights of the week. Then, with some deranged form of a schedule I ran at least five miles a day, a minimum six days a week. Burying myself in long nights of dancing, laughing, and pulling lame pranks, any which could have had me arrested more times than my DUI and my supposed runaway excursion in my teen years combined. Running while still intoxicated was common for me in my mornings. My living arrangements were just as numerous and unstable as my sobriety. This was the numbing cocktail of my existence.

Roller skating or riding bikes to bars with back packs full of beer, locking cab drivers out of their cabs while they stopped to pick up their nightly caffeine, and overtaking their walkie-talkies until they promised to drive my friends and me home for free was a part of my nightly amusement. Drinking with people I worked with gave me the benefits of communal hangovers, so there was ample sympathy in the rotation of hugging the porcelain throne in between helping customers.

When the local bars became boring, we figured out we had enough girls to split a limo on the weekends. This meant a mobile bar that drove us through San Francisco to a much larger spectrum of dance clubs. Then, the limo drove us home safely while we all passed out, piled on top of each other in disarray. The majority of our group stayed pretty consistent and new relationships caused brief absences that were hardly ever noticed.

Going out and drinking with the girls took precedence over finding mister right and settling down. Bringing men into the mix meant bringing in accountabilities and commitments I wasn't responsible enough to handle at the time. My fickleness worked for my anesthetized living standards.

By the time I turned twenty, my mom was in her late thirties, raising two more children in their elementary years. There were nights when she would come out with my friends or just hung out with me wherever I was living at the time. Somewhere around this time, my mom became my peer. It was the numb leading the blind on an equal playing field. I didn't look up to her as much as I saw her as one of the women in my life trying to find their way, whatever that was.

A few months ago I had dinner with my friend Dave, who I was very connected to in my twenties and also had worked with my mom at the Sonoma County Prison. He reminded me of his worst night ever in seventeen years of being a lieutenant at the facility.

It was early morning when he started his shift. He found me sitting in the holding area, hiding my swollen, red face in my hands, and sobbing like a new widow that has just lost the love of her life. He remembered praying it wasn't me. But as he walked closer, he stopped in front of me and looked down.

His face . . . that was the most sobering part of that whole night.

On Thursday nights from Memorial Day to Labor Day, the local merchants had a market along three or four blocks of Fourth Street in downtown Santa Rosa. The brewery, where I bartended, had a booth selling oysters. A few of us from the bar worked there as well.

Drinking with the girls at night and running numerous miles during the day was my lifestyle at the time. My body fat was low and getting drunk didn't usually cost me very much. Still, I was known to be able to hold my own with at least a couple shots backed up by a pitcher.

On this particular night, I had run earlier in the day and rushed to work at the oyster booth without eating anything of real substance. A girlfriend met me at the booth and after work we went upstairs to one of the bars to go dancing. We knew the bouncers and bartenders from working out at the gym or working with them downtown in the bar scene.

When Lisa and I got upstairs around 10 p.m., we noticed the crowd was different. We recognized the staff, but we didn't really recognize any of the patrons. Growing up in Santa Rosa, which wasn't a huge town, made it easy to run into someone you had grown up with. We went to the bar, got our first beers of the night, and headed out to the dance floor. Before the first song was barely over, a bouncer caught us with our drinks on the dance floor, scolded us, and told us to put our full bottles on the surrounding ledges. We didn't even think twice about it as we were familiar with our surroundings and continued dancing. Eventually, we went back to our beers, finished them, and went to the bar for our traditional shot of tequila.

From this point on until I was arrested, my story is told through Lisa's words. I remember nothing from here on.

As Lisa tells it, I decided I could pour my own shot of tequila better than our bartender friends and proceeded to climb over the bar to pour whatever tickled my fancy. Lisa and the bartenders tried to grab me, but they said I was as slippery as a well-greased pig. They could barely get the bottles out of my hands before I started pouring complimentary refills in any glass on the bar that wasn't full. The bouncers had to carry me out over their shoulders to keep me from trying to grab drinks from innocent bystanders on my way to the curb.

From here, Lisa had to catch up with me as I ran down the street to another bar. There I ran into an old friend that I had dated for a very short time and proceeded to yell gibberish at him. When Lisa tried to pull me away, I turned on her and demanded my keys. After a battle, Lisa gave them up as long as I promised to sleep in my car. She lost me before midnight.

At 5:30 the next morning, I woke up in my car in the bottom floor of the Macy's parking lot in the mall. Not remembering anything from the night before, I proceeded to drive home.

The sun wasn't up yet and it was still very dark when I entered the freeway. The highway patrol said they had their lights on me for a while before I pulled off the freeway at my exit to go home. They had to call out over their loud speaker for me to pull over in the Round Table parking lot. I was completely oblivious as to why they were bugging me to pull over. When the officer came to my window and asked me if I had been drinking, I answered him honestly and told him of my one drink.

When he asked me to step out of the car so I could see how I parked, I saw that I had pulled onto one of the dividers in the parking lot. And when he asked me to say the alphabet backwards, I told him I couldn't even do that sober. My only options were to breathe into a breathalyzer or to do a blood test back at the prison where my mom, Dave, and all of our friends worked. I didn't vote for my second option. I blew a .12 and was read my rights. Tears flowed down my face faster than a waterfall fed by the melting ice from a long winter's nap.

The officers said my story didn't make sense from what I remembered and what I blew. They asked me if I wanted to take a drug test to see what inhibited the alcohol and without hesitation I sobbed my declination because I knew I hadn't taken anything . . . voluntarily.

When we arrived at the prison, we were greeted by officers that had been to picnics and functions with my family and me in the past few years. My mom was coming into work at 7 a.m. and was soon going to kill me. The women that fingerprinted me and took my pictures all knew me. I kept crying and trying to hug them. They kept scolding me to stop. They put me in a cell to calm down, telling me that once I did they would let me call my mother. It seemed like forever because every time I knocked on the door, I started balling again. They let me out to make my call.

"Hello, Ma?"

"Christina, why are you calling me from my work?"

Good old caller I.D.

"Hang up, I will call you right back."

As soon as I hung up I heard the phone ring at the counter right next to me. The woman that answered explained to my mom that she had to come get me because I was trying to hug everyone. I heard her apologize to my mom for not being more compassionate and then handed me the phone.

"Hello," I started sobbing again.

"Christina, you're going to get them into trouble. Stop trying to touch everyone and stop crying or they will put you back in a cell. Do you hear me?"

I looked up at the lady and bit my lip to try to stop the crying. "Uh-huh."

"I'll be down there in a minute. Stop crying or else they will not let me take you." She inhaled her cigarette and hung up.

As I turned around, Dave was standing behind me. The look of stern anger and disappointment was set on his face. He pointed me into a cell without a word. Once I was in there, he disappointedly asked, "Why? What happened? Why didn't you call me?"

In my blubbering, I told him what I remembered.

"Christina, did you take the drug test? It sounds like you were slipped a roofie. I know you can drink more than one beer without losing it and something doesn't sound right."

"No, I didn't. Can I now?"

"It's too late," he said sadly. "You already checked in. You have to have it done when you first got here. It's too late now. You should have called me. I am so disappointed in you. Have you called your mom?" he asked sternly.

"Yeah, she's coming." I blubbered.

"You have got to stop crying. Otherwise they will keep you in here. Clean up your face and compose yourself."

As we walked out, my mom was waiting for me at the counter.

"Let's go." She thanked the ladies and scurried me out so fast she didn't have time to beat me.

We drove home in silence, stopping only to get my car which was half parked onto the cement dividers, my tires intertwined with the bush. I followed my mom home in my car, drowsy, nauseous, and achy. I started to crash heavily. We called the bartender from the night before and he authenticated my prior night's consumption, bringing to light the hole in my memory.

As my mom put me to bed she asked, "Why didn't you take the drug test?"

"It just mortified me when he asked me, Ma. It was the farthest from my mind that I would have been drugged. I'm coming down though like I was."

My avoidance in dealing with my past was armored with angst and fleeing, dodging any form of consequence. My peers, at the time, were answering the questions of "What do I do?" and "What am I worth?" Defining my identity was more difficult, especially when I really wasn't that interested in finding out the answer.

By this time, my relationship with my mother masked over my anguish of what I thought was a lack of a childhood. This turned into a drive to forget and to make excuses for my own actions. And so became the birth of my story, my evolution of my excuses for being so cold and relentless.

Running was my life force. I had ideal runs for each town in Sonoma County, accommodating my long run days and my quickies. The only thing I lived for in those days was running. It was my movement, my release. Occasionally I would acquire a running partner with the same running style as me, but they were always short lived. I lost touch with Selena after high school and Shawn, a girl I waited tables with, married and became a mommy. Sharing schedules turned into a bigger focus than the run at hand. Running on my own became my biggest freedom, my escape out of any hardships that I had manifested for myself.

The days of burying my head in pillows, sobbing my life away were over. Climbing steep mountains of various grades developed into my greatest drug of choice. The cadence of my heart harmonized with my feet pounding up and down the dirt paths and desolate country roads, always pulling me forward.

Out of the numerous houses and rooms I rented in my twenties, the house out in the countryside by Sebastopol was my favorite. It was located on a long stretch of silent country road filled with different grades of hills. One of my roommates was a drummer in a band and the owner of a large snake. Another frequented our rooftop to hit buckets of balls and to have camp-outs with his mattress pulled out from his bedroom. I came home once to the roommates washing our dishes with our hose in one of the large Rubbermaid trash cans we had used out on the porch. At some point, the drummer lost his snake and ended up finding it in one of his cinder blocks that held up his bed a few months later. The comings and goings in that house were constant. There was always someone there or something happening that was interesting to watch. It seemed like I would catch glimpses of the action as I was passing through between classes or work.

My busyness eventually caught up with me. When my world stopped spinning for a moment, I realized my productivity didn't have much to show for itself. My forward began to rotate backward. And, my band aid had finally started to lose its stickiness. Being careless eventually became unattractive.

Somewhere along the path, my story grew heftier, full of confusion and grief. It became second nature for me to practice and recite my lines for my dramatic sob story. My fishbowl was filled with murky water and I had become so accustomed to it that my clarity was absolutely distorted.

I had become complacent. Manipulating relationships was my sole means of survival. Fear of rejection had spun me into endless loops of unhealthy relationships that repeatedly played 'the come here, go away' game. With my reckless behavior it was commonplace to beat down others for my own benefit. I found myself alone. Ridiculously alone . . . an unnecessary beating of wills.

Towards the end of my twenties, I became tired of the chaos. My addiction to drama didn't excite me anymore; it just created more blind tragedy to recover from, on a bigger scale, at a later time. I developed a new escape plan.

It was time to get serious, get married, and have children. Being a wife and mother would make me responsible like everyone else. My white picket fence would appear. Everything behind closed doors would be perfect. There was no way I would ever let my child be hurt like I was and my husband would give me the nurturing family I never had.

What I learned quickly though, was that cycles continue to spin in the same direction unless you break their course. My solution only brought me another escape route that caught up with me soon after my son's first birthday. I had only been married for two years and my marriage was over. This devastating realization was my breaking point. I had failed.

All the abandonment and trust I had never felt secure with growing up, had let me down again. I had sabotaged yet another relationship, but on a much grander scale this time. While I started my divorce process, Chris and I moved into another home. I dealt with my grief by diving into work. Chris was small enough that I could throw blankets and pillows under my desk with toys for him to play and to nap.

A co-worker had watched me lose a drastic amount of weight, lose all interest in looking presentable, and observed me tote my toddler to and from work at all hours of the day and night. She had gone to this spiritual boot camp type of training in southern California and started hounding me to look into it for myself.

I saw her as this flawless, wealthy woman who had never been violated as a child and had biological parents that were still happily married. There was no way a feel-good, resort-type of retreat was going to magically make all my pain go away. But, after a few months of her prodding, I cautiously looked into it. The course was a week long and my superficial concerns consisted of leaving Christopher and work.

At first glance, I knew this would be the type of place that would force me to rewrite my script that I had manifested into a love-hate relationship for so long. My story had begun to give me a shorter and shorter gratification period. My honeymoon phase with it had far exceeded its threshold. I knew my destructive cycle consisted of my story and part of me was afraid to let go of this enabling crutch.

From the moment I knew I was pregnant with Chris, I vowed to never let him down and to always protect him. I had failed at both. I had failed at keeping our family together and I had begun to yell at him for things a toddler should not have been responsible for, crushing his little spirit. If there was the slightest chance that a training could help me break down my story, purge it, and never be weighed down by it again, then I had to redeem myself for my sanity and for the love I had for my son.

The training was the hardest, yet at the same time the lightest, work I had ever done for myself. Coming out of it I felt a hundred pounds lighter. I spooked myself into not succumbing to my old patterns. Daily, I worked at and watched what triggered my life. I saw how losing my temper or feeding into gossip and nonsense created a domino effect that quickly had me falling back into my old patterns. I also noticed that my environment played a major factor in how fluid my days ran. The more I stayed away from drama, the less addicting it became.

It's very important to me to surround myself with peers who can catch me in my downtimes. They remind me that I know better and to hold myself accountable. The weight of the story went away and what replaced it was a conscious responsibility, which is much more comfortable to carry. It is definitely more rewarding when you acknowledge that your own ego is the culprit to your insanity.

I have made amends with my protectors that have let me down in this lifetime. I don't carry around blame and anger for those that I think have wronged me. I use the tools that I acquired in my daily life to contribute in the best way I can.

I still get triggered. I still feel let down at times. Normally though, if I can just hold out for a moment to respond instead of reacting, I can see my blessing waiting for me at the end of the day.

MY NANA

That one last shot's a Permanent Vacation
And how high can you fly with broken wings?
Life's a journey not a destination
And I just can't tell just what tomorrow brings

"Amazing" by Aerosmith

Once I was asked what I thought were the top ten highest qualities of the human spirit. I came up with; unconditional love, patience, humility, service, high intention, accommodating, compassionate, cuddly, honesty, and strength. Then I was asked if that embodied anyone I knew. My answer was my grandmother or as I knew her, my nana. In Sicilian, grandparents are known as Nanu and Nana.

My mother's mother was born in Madison Wisconsin on July 28, 1913. Josephine Grace Gianquinto, my nana, was one of nine children. As a child, my nana worked on her parents' farm with her four sisters and four brothers. She attended school for only three years, barely learning how to read and write. At thirteen, she started her first job at a woolen hosiery factory making nylons.

My grandfather was her neighbor and childhood friend, whom she married at the age of twenty eight and became Josephine Grace Licari. Both of my grandparents were Sicilian.

When my nanu enlisted in the Army, they moved to Texas. My nana, not knowing anyone, waited tables while my nanu was stationed in New Guinea during World War II. In one letter she wrote to Nanu, she proclaimed how happy she was at her new job. She noticed and thought it was odd that in Texas her customers always seemed to forget their nickels and pennies on the tables. She wrote how nice her fellow employees were to her, always helping to clear off her tables. My nanu wrote back to her explaining that the left behind change was called tips and that the other waiters and bus boys were stealing from her.

When he returned from the war, they moved to Rockford, Illinois where my nana gave birth to her first of four children. Her eldest daughter passed away after only a couple of days on earth due to spinal issues. Uncle Mike, Sisi Josie, and Uncle Joe were born in Illinois. When Uncle Joe was three, my nanu moved his growing family to Pittsburg, California. At first, when they arrived in California Nanu worked in a factory to support his family. Eventually he became a bartender and worked for the Hotel and Culinary Workers Union. His shifts were long, lasting into the early morning hours the majority of the time. Gambling, drinking, and women were where most of his income was spent.

My nana raised her three toddlers, miscarried her fifth pregnancy, and then had my mother. With family finances dwindling, my nana went back to work, leaving her children to tend themselves when they weren't in school. She took random jobs at the cannery, the local newspaper, in the cafeteria at the steel mill, and at the banquet hall at the Elks Lodge. She always made sure her children were fed, clothed, and had a roof over their head.

By the time I was born, her husband was the town ladies' man, her two eldest boys were in the military, her eldest daughter was married with her first child, and my mom was still a teenager. My nana worked, dealt with my mom who was in and out of juvenile hall, and raised me.

Nana would lie down with my cousin and me humming Italian melodies or make up songs while she lightly tickled our faces with the tips of her chubby wrinkled fingers to put us to sleep. Her voice was deep and worn. When and if, she ever rose her voice, her velvety tone was still reassuring. Her scent was Opium mixed with tomato sauce; Vicks vapor rub, and Lysol. As a toddler, these smells were comforting as I climbed up her voluptuous body to get a hug or a kiss. There were three of us cousins that were close in age, and Nana would call us her dollies. We absolutely adored her.

Nana crocheted a blanket for each grandchild, making them unique by choosing our favorite colors. Mine was pink, lime green, and yellow. When we were of school age, she taught each of us how to crochet little flower book marks and sew, while she mended our clothes. Nana called me her favorite. She would say that she didn't love me more than the others; I just needed her more than the others. She would say that they had stability and that she was my stability.

My nana was an amazing cook and eating in her kitchen was like having your own restaurant. If we wanted pizza, she would make us a pizza. If we wanted any kind of pasta, raviolis, meatballs, chicken fried steak, or fried zucchini flowers, she made them for us from scratch. For the holidays, she made her Italian cookies, cuchidades (Italian fig Newton's), meringues, biscotti's, and muscardinis. They all filled old oversized popcorn tins to their brims, which she tried to hide in her closet to keep us out of them. My nanu, who was also a cookieaholic, would always convince her to pull them out after meals. Quickly, we were keen to her hiding place.

Mornings smelled of fried spaghetti and eggs. The house always smelled of spaghetti sauce as the cooking process would start in early in the morning and stew throughout the whole day. Her sauce was rich, warm, and soothing pulling from the sweet tomatoes, pungent garlic, and perfect balances of rosemary, thyme, and oregano. Sounds of bubbling stewed tomatoes filled the air when she lifted the lid to skim off the top.

What engrossed Nana most in conversations was what you were interested in eating for your next meal, so she could start her preparations immediately. Conversations at every meal also centered on what we wanted at the next meal, among other things.

I spent a majority of my time with her before I started my schooling. My mom and I lived in San Francisco, after she left Bill the first time, and Nana lived in Pittsburg, then later in Hayward. When my mom worked, it was more convenient if I stayed at Nana's house for extended periods of time. I had a routine at Nana's. We woke up at a certain time, ate three full large meals a day, and I played outside with other grandkids who were visiting. I saw my family members more often. Nana loved to play cards; she taught me gin, solitaire, and war. She kept a board on a side table for her puzzles.

Our afternoons were spent at the table close to the kitchen sitting on her recliner, watching her soaps. I loved painting Nana's nails and rubbing her hands to alleviate her arthritis. She had a nasty habit of picking at her cuticles. I would rub lotion on them to stop the cracking and the bleeding at night when she would watch her game shows.

As I got older and entered school, I saw less and less of her. While my mom was with Bill, we didn't celebrate holidays, so we didn't see my mom's family during that time. When I started driving I would go see her. I delighted in bringing my friends to meet this amazing woman.

My nanu passed away when I turned twenty leaving my nana with no one to cook for. They were married for over fifty years. I didn't find out about his ways until after they had both passed away. Nana knew how Nanu was, never letting her children in on any of his instability. She just handled it. When I was younger, she would have me read to her, instead of her reading to me. Never once did she let on that I was the better reader. Yet, whenever I needed anything mended or made for me, she knew how to do it. She was the epitome of grace and ease.

I never heard Nana complain. She just resolved her issue. Her selfless nature was of service wherever she went. In my twenties, Nana was easy to talk to. She was free of judgment when it came to me. She was alone and she missed Nanu. My aunt, her eldest daughter, would visit the most often, which gave me a little bit of comfort. A part of me wished I could spend more time with her to escape my self-inflicted chaos.

When I found out I was pregnant with Christopher, I altered my efforts to spend more time with Nana. By then, she was in a skilled nursing facility; a breast cancer survivor living with dementia. She lived the end of her life clear of dependence on her family, living on her own until she went into the hospital. It was as if I was hoping for her to rub off on me.

My mother didn't interact with me during my pregnancy. Not talking to me was her method of proving her point to whatever she felt was relevant at the time. I sat with Nana and asked her questions about her childhood. I loved her stories. I loved her memories. I watched her revert more and more into a jovial state as I ate lunch with her in her little nursing home, where someone else cooked for her.

Nana passed away peacefully in her sleep less than two months before Christopher was born. She was 88 years old. She survived ten years after Nanu passed away. I never saw her cry, or show sadness, yet I knew her absence of serving others left her with a loss of direction. Her self-worth, her life work, was to nurture and protect. Without that she was a lost soul. Not being helpful left her helpless.

I was blessed to have her in my life. She always stood by me even when I felt I didn't deserve it. Her unconditional love was my mountain. Her patience was my saving grace. My respect for her will always be held in the highest of regards. My grandma was the greatest Spirit I have ever known. I aspire to master her ten qualities and each morning when I create my day, I remind myself of them…unconditional love, patience, humility, service, high intention, accommodating, compassionate, cuddly, honesty, and strength.

AT THIS POINT IN MY LIFE

"To thine own self be true."

Act 1, scene 3, 78–82, from Hamlet

A t this point in my life, I have found my peace. My will of accountability to ever improve in all aspects of my life drives me to wake up each morning grateful for what I have, for what I have accomplished, and for what I am capable of giving to others. My awareness of a need gives me plenty of opportunities to be accountable and to contribute in the best way I know how.

I have a conscious choice to be active in the uplifting of my community. I choose my integrity. I live in my faith that everything presented to me will be of its purest intention. God gives me opportunities so that I can see my miracle at the end of the day. What happens for me, I am thankful for. I am blessed, not believing in luck. I do not rely on random acts of chance, forgetting that my soul source and provider always blesses me for my greater good. I claim my divine right, falling back to my one and only provider.

My journey has been painful at times, my lessons have been large. I am grateful for them, for great strength has emerged from them. I have made my choice to keep running forward, wiping off my wounded knees covered with disillusionment and ego. I live in amazement of how far I have come; knowing in my heart there is so much more yet to do.

My highest version of myself is ever being manifested through my service to others, free from any attachments. This agreement that has been made in each and every one of us to seek our own truth has empowered me to forgive and to accept that what one does is always right for them. I remind myself that my attachment to their actions keeps me from improving mine.

I love my life, it has brought me here. I wake up every morning and ask myself, "How far will I run today?"

Author Bio

CHRISTINA BAIRD was born and raised in Northern California, where she has made it her life work to be of service through accountability in her communities. Christina understands people, local businesses, and their missions. She connects all through humanistic marketing as she creates an awareness of a need. She believes a community has the conscious choice to contribute, or find avenues that can. In addition, Christina serves on the Vacaville Community Services Commission appointed by the mayor, is acting President of the Vacaville Chapter, serving all of Solano County, Optimist club and owns two public relations and marketing companies. Christina volunteers her time to Solano County's Office of Education's Career Technical Education high school program and facilitates an accountability and contribution luncheon, keeping local business owners informed of any community needs.

Her passion for running is in alignment for how she lives her life in a day-to-day environment. Creating a space to always go a little bit farther, accomplishing feats that were once thought to be unattainable, she appears to continually train for life's marathon. This book is her journey as a committed student of compassion and growth, who loves and serves to the best of her ability.